MW01280028

SALE$ COACHING

Four key steps to achieving your goals and objectives in sales

DÍO ASTACIO

SALES COACHING

Four key steps to achieving your goals and objectives in sales

by Dío Astacio

ISBN: 978-1-942991-25-0

Published by
Editorial RENUEVO

www.EditorialRenuevo.com
info@EditorialRenuevo.com

CONTENTS

Introduction   9

Chapter 1: Real Confidence   15

Developing Trust   19

Six Ways to Win Confidence   21

The Empathy That Blunders   35

Knowing the Temperaments   39

Chapter 2: In-Depth Analysis   45

Searching for Real Needs   52

How to Perform an In-Depth Analysis   57

Reasons for Buying: the Concept   59

Four Areas of Essential Questions   63

Take Notes   82

Chapter 3: Product Presentation   **95**

Five Recommendations for Making
a Presentation Interesting   101

CHAPTER 4: Aggressive Closing   **119**

Three Characteristics of an Aggressive Close   133

Manage Your Own Emotions   147

Don't Forget About Customer Service   150

DEDICATION

*To Melody, Daniela, and Camila, with a desire for them to
learn how to reach their maximum potential.*

*To my wife Evelyn, who listens attentively to all of her
customers and associates.*

To my father Darío Astacio, a born salesman.

To my mother Milka Pacheco, my life coach.

To all my customers, for being the source of my knowledge.

To my friends in sales.

INTRODUCTION

Sales Coaching

*Hello my friend, and welcome to
Sales Coaching.*

Is it possible to become a good salesperson in a short period of time? If I told you Yes, would you believe me? *Sales Coaching* is a book designed for those who wish to try their hand at sales and business but don't know how. This book is also designed to increase the knowledge of those who have dedicated a large part of their lives to this career. My aim is to make sales something easy so that those without prior experience may be able to follow four key steps to achieve their objectives.

The act of selling is a complex matter. And if you were to review the manuals and books that have been written about this subject down through the years, you would find a great number of recommendations (certainly valid ones) that can make sales more complicated. Not that they are wrong. But based on all these ideas and my experience, I would like to share four steps that will get you on your way to becoming a successful salesperson, or consultant.

There are many products that don't sell, not necessarily

because they are bad products, but because many salespeople fail to take the correct approach—and that will drive away a potential customer. Following the correct order in the sales process will benefit both the seller and the customer. Many times this order is ignored. A seller cannot start right off presenting a product without having first gained the confidence of the customer.

I worked as a salesman for a long time. I sold many types of consumer products and services. As the years passed, I occupied positions of increasing responsibility that were directly involved in the management of sales forces. As a result, I am interested in helping correct the typical mistakes that even experienced salespeople make, causing them to fall short of their objectives, despite the time and effort they spend. These mistakes ultimately reduce their sales potential and affect their results.

You can use whatever strategy you prefer. In the end, sales are always made and people always buy, but the point is that the percentage of results will not be the same. I encourage you to practice these four steps, and you will see the results you so desire.

CHAPTER ONE

REAL CONFIDENCE

Where there is no trust, everything that follows will be short-lived. Trust is the basis of every good relationship.

Sales Coaching

DEVELOPING TRUST

The first step toward making a sale is winning people's confidence. Nothing will happen if people don't trust you. Confidence is the first thing you must sell. If prospects feel you are not a trustworthy person when they see you, they will look for thousands of reasons not to buy from you. Looking at it another way, people find reasons to buy from someone they trust.

Imagine that you have just walked into a shoe store. You are met by a salesman who inspires your confidence. You feel comfortable because you believe that what this salesman is telling you is true. He treats you with amazing kindness, goes over details, and fosters a favorable environment in the process. Later, you will come up with several reasons to buy from this person, even if you don't like the shoes.

Confidence is a determining factor. If you pull into a gas station to fill up your car but don't take the cap off your gas tank, the gasoline will never go in. It doesn't matter how much you pay or how hard you try, you cannot pump gas if the cap is still on. Confidence is like that gas cap: it needs to be opened so that any information you want to take to a customer will be able to get in, and so he or she, in turn, will be able to retain and use that information. If a salesperson does not take the "confidence" cap off, then the customer will not open his mind to the product that is being offered, no matter how cheap or good the product may be.

◇◇◇◇◇◇◇◇◇◇◇◇◇◇◇◇◇◇◇◇◇◇◇◇◇◇
A common mistake among salespeople is thinking only about selling a product
◇◇◇◇◇◇◇◇◇◇◇◇◇◇◇◇◇◇◇◇◇◇◇◇◇◇

A common mistake among salespeople is thinking only about selling a product; they focus on the money, on immediately describing their product or service, on explaining how it will be useful and why the customer should buy it. They forget they are speaking with human beings who need someone who first of all will listen to them, observe them, and help them as the persons they are, not just because they want to sell them something. The salesperson who focuses only on selling and making money is not a salesperson who inspires confidence.

In the following pages, I wish to present some techniques used to gain trust, and give a broader explanation of what the subject of confidence is all about.

SIX WAYS TO WIN CONFIDENCE

1. FROM THE ABUNDANCE OF THE HEART

The first way to win someone's confidence is to check on your inner self. You must take a look at your values, your priorities, your very self. No one can project a confidence they lack, for that would be hypocrisy. From time to time, you might take some people by surprise, but it would be difficult for you to become a seller who inspires trust if your inner self seeks to fool others.

It has always been believed that the act of selling consists in the following: I give you a product, and regardless of what happens with it, you pay me a sum of money, and everything ends there. That is not a noble sale; therefore, it is not a proper sale. A sale should not end when the customer takes the product; in reality, that should be the beginning of a good sale.

A sale must not have a feeling of taking advantage, because that would turn the entire process into a mere fraud.

A sale should produce relationships that will last a lifetime, and that simply cannot happen without trust. Therefore, sellers should examine their own values, their inner self, and the essence of their being.

Good salespeople should think about what is their true motivation behind selling a product or service. They should ask themselves the following questions: When I go out to sell, am I doing it because I want to receive a benefit while at the same time wanting to meet needs in the life of someone else? Or am I only interested in having customers buy from me without caring what happens in their lives? Should that person also receive a real benefit from my sale, or should I alone benefit from it? If salespeople's thoughts leave the buyer's benefit out of the picture, then they must totally change their way of thinking.

◇◇◇◇◇◇◇◇◇◇◇◇◇◇◇◇◇◇◇◇◇◇◇◇◇◇
The big markets all strive to obtain their customers' complete satisfaction
◇◇◇◇◇◇◇◇◇◇◇◇◇◇◇◇◇◇◇◇◇◇◇◇◇◇

When you sell a product, the absolute satisfaction of the buyer must be your first priority. All the great companies of the world aim to achieve this: the total satisfaction of their customers. If you head to a major chain in the United States (or other developed country) and buy any product, you can be sure that you may return that product—weeks or even months later—if it did not meet your expectations. That store will refund your money entirely because it understands that a sale is an agreement: the store offers its customers a product that completely satisfies them, and the store benefits from the customers' satisfaction. If that satisfaction fails to happen in the sales process, then the agreement is void because one of the parties has been defrauded. Civilization itself aims toward this goal. The big markets all strive to obtain their customers' complete satisfaction.

This is a good moment to reflect and take a look at your inner self: Do I really want to give my best for someone else? Do I really want to offer the best product? If the customer is not entirely satisfied, would I be willing to completely refund their money? These questions are very pertinent and vital to your being able to project trustworthiness toward others.

2. PROJECTING OUTWARD APPEARANCE

Once you have reviewed your inner self, it is time to move on to the second phase: reviewing your exterior self. When you look at yourself in the mirror, do you see someone you really would buy from? Is the way you look consistent with what you are selling? The way you project yourself physically, in terms of personal presence, should be consistent with the product you are trying to sell. For example, a salesman offering plumbing products must not look like a lawyer; he must look like someone knowledgeable in his area. To the customer, you are a plumber, and you know what you offer. The same principle applies to lawyers (who should not look like plumbers or mechanics) or doctors (who must carry themselves so as to inspire confidence in their patients).

What you project with your presence is very important because that ultimately ends up being linked with the product.

People who do multilevel marketing have a very interesting way of presenting themselves, because they know they are projecting themselves toward a future sale. These independent businessmen and women sell dreams to people and tell them that all will be well and that multilevel marketing produces a lot of money. Therefore, they should dress like people who produce or are on their way to producing money.

Personal appearance can project confidence—or the lack of it—depending on what is being offered for sale. In this sense, it is vital for you to follow the rules of behavior and dress pertaining to your industry.

Your scent is another point. No one likes doing business with someone who smells bad, has bad breath, or has an unkempt appearance. If you offer tattoos for sale, then a certain amount of sloppiness is normal for those who wear them, because that is a community that seeks to project a sense of rebelliousness. But if you are selling something else, the general rule is that your body should look cared for. Why is this relevant? Because customers will judge that if you are incapable of taking care of your own self, you will be even less able to give them good service or benefit them. They may conclude that since you have not paid attention to your own life, you will not pay attention to theirs.

My advice is that you take good care of your body, your hair, your fingernails, and your teeth. Make sure to iron your clothing and wear the appropriate footwear. This is an

> **Personal appearance can project confidence — or the lack of it**

important point for women because many times their shoes do not go with their labor. A comfortable pair of executive-style heels is a good match for women who are employed in the sale of services or products to the executive class. If they are street merchants, then it is logical for their shoes to be comfortable and appropriate to the products they are selling. I have seen lady sales agents who visit doctors wearing very high, expensive heels, and likewise, I have seen women who are in executive sales in large multinational corporations wearing athletic shoes.

Everything you display with regard to your appearance has an impact on the confidence you inspire because you may be strengthening or weakening your image in the customer's eyes.

3. THE COMPLETE SET OF TOOLS

Thirdly, I will go over the tools or instruments salespeople need according to the product they are representing.

In the previous point, I dealt with something related to this, for example, that an engineer must look like what he or she is: an engineer. They wear boots, hard hats, jeans or slacks, a measuring tape on their waists, and a level. The same goes for doctors, lawyers, medical sales agents, or insurance salespeople with their briefcases. Regardless of what commodity or service you are selling, you should look the part according to what you are offering.

The tools of the trade are part of the sale

The tools of the trade are part of the sale.

I also mentioned the importance of dressing correctly and having good hygiene. But now I will go over the instruments that complement that uniform. Let's say, for example, you hire a plumber. He shows up at your door offering his services well-dressed, clean (though he may get dirty while working), and greets you courteously. Once he starts working, however, he asks you for tools: "Do you have pliers?" "Would you happen to have a wrench?" Tell me, would you trust this plumber? Of course not. You would lose confidence in him because he lacks the tools of the trade.

The tools of the trade are part of the sale. If you go out selling but your briefcase looks messy and you don't have the documents or tools you need, you will project a lack of organization, which will make others lose confidence in you. The customer will think you don't know what you're doing. It's like a doctor without a stethoscope, or a book merchant without books. However, the more these tools are available, well-presented and well-cared-for, the more confidence you will be able to inspire in your customers.

I want to ask you some questions. Do you have all the tools you'll need when a customer comes to you: calculator, pens, forms, measuring instruments, catalogs? Do you have all your products at hand? Can you show that you can be trusted, that you have everything you need to do a good job filling the needs of your customer? If you are going out today to sell products or provide services, ask yourself these questions.

4. THE IMPORTANCE OF WORDS AND KNOWLEDGE

Until now, I have dealt with three important points on the subject of confidence: how it is felt (how it is projected from within); how it is seen (how it is projected outward); and whether you have all the necessary tools. Now I will approach the subject of words and knowledge. What you say and how you say it—speaks volumes about your professionalism.

People will constantly evaluate your words. Salespeople who don't know what they're talking about, who don't know everything about their product, or who don't care to keep their language appropriate to what's being offered—it's practically impossible for them to inspire confidence. The words you use and how you use them will determine to a large extent the amount of confidence your customers will have toward you. It is for this reason that you must know your product and be knowledgeable about everything related to the product's industry. You should know everything about your company. You should observe your customers in depth to learn more about them. Take great care how you use your words, how you communicate and how you address others. These things begin with the following three points.

The first point is the subject of formality. In basic

conversation, respectful forms of address like sir or ma'am are used to establish a certain distance between parties and to indicate that the subject is a person who deserves respect. It is very common for some salespeople to use more informal language with someone they have just met to try to establish a rapport between them, without having received prior permission from the customer. Therefore, the language used in communicating with customers, regardless of what you sell, should always be prudent and respectful. Regardless of how straightforward or emotional a person may seem, don't think that you are selling to a friend. You are not selling to a friend; you are selling to a customer, so you must always maintain your distance. In a sense, this distance suggests professionalism and respect.

> **The words you use and how you use them will determine to a large extent the amount of confidence your customers will have toward you**

The second point is the technical aspect. Once you have carried yourself with professionalism and respect (by maintaining your distance, even if you've been working with your customer for two years), you should know what you're talking about in regard to your merchandise. If you don't know the technical details about your products, it will be very difficult to inspire confidence. When you visit your doctor, he is almost certain to use medical terms. Regardless of how plainly he may express the information so you can understand it, he will use vocabulary that shows what he knows and who he is. You probably don't know many of those words, but you trust your doctor fully and respect what he says. The same is true for a lawyer, mechanic, or a parts salesperson.

It's not that the language they use is so fine, but that it is appropriate to the career they are in.

An insurance salesman, for example, should know the meaning of technical terms such as policy, risk, and premium, since these are common words in the insurance market. It is possible the customer may not know anything about these terms, and the sales representative may have to explain each of them. Nevertheless, the customer will observe that the salesman knows his trade.

◇◇◇◇◇◇◇◇◇◇◇◇◇◇◇◇◇◇◇◇◇◇◇◇◇

Know the meaning of technical terms

◇◇◇◇◇◇◇◇◇◇◇◇◇◇◇◇◇◇◇◇◇◇◇◇◇

A multilevel marketer should know the words that

form part of that industry's glossary: upline, downline, kit, line of sponsorship, and networks. It is of utmost importance to know the industry language, the job language, regardless of what you sell. The seller who neglects to do so cannot project confidence. If a car salesman tries to sell me a vehicle without using car-related language and terms, he won't get the sale. I could not have confidence in him, because he would not have demonstrated possessing enough knowledge.

On one occasion, while visiting a friend, an insurance salesman came by. (I worked as a salesman for many years, so I know the insurance market well; I managed sales forces for important companies in my country.) It was a bitter experience for this young salesman because my friend, who is also employed in the same sector, began asking questions about the international health product the young man was offering. He seemed to be newly hired, yet he had taken to the streets without researching or having any knowledge of the technical language used in this market. My friend wanted to know who were the reinsurers of this particular product. The young man didn't even know what a reinsurer was. He also could not explain much about the company that managed the network of affiliates on the international level, saying only, "They have hospitals and clinics in the United States and other parts of the world." He also didn't know that the insured had to prequalify to use their services. We ended up giving the young man a talk about international insurance. It was quite embarrassing for him.

Knowledge generates confidence—but so do the right words and their proper use. This is why you should check up on your language every day. A good way to do this is by recording yourself, both on audio and video, to be able to listen to yourself and review the sound and the words of your vocabulary. You will be able to watch not only your verbal language but also your body language, gestures, voice modulation, and the confidence you project. By doing this, you will know if you would really buy from someone like yourself.

> **Knowledge generates confidence—but so do the right words and their proper use**

Remember you should try to use language that is professional, respectful, and warm—but with the appropriate distance and technical knowledge. And above all else, it must be capable of inspiring confidence in the person you're speaking to.

5. EMPATHY

To achieve empathy, you have to be careful, when trying

to find something in common with another person, that you don't end up rubbing them the wrong way.

To empathize is to feel empathy, to identify with another person. It is the act of looking for something in common between two people.

Nobody buys from someone they don't like, so you should try to be liked by your customer. But empathy goes above and beyond simply being liked by someone. For example, it is not appropriate to try selling a product to a person who is going through a difficult time in life and try to achieve empathy by talking about a subject like golf. Empathizing does not mean talking about golf, finances, basketball, or anything like that; empathizing means identifying yourself with the other person in such a way as to discern what that person is feeling in that moment.

Empathy has two components: the cognitive component, that is related to capturing mental processes, and the emotional component, that is linked to the emotional reaction of the other person. You can get to where you recognize the stimuli and emotional expressions of your customers and interpret them.

Empathy has been a subject of study in several disciplines such as theology, philosophy, psychology, and neuroscience. Although it shares common attributes with sympathy, it is not the same thing. Sympathy leans more toward kindness and grace, toward the establishment of certain common ideas. It's like saying, "I like this person," or "He's a nice guy." Empathy, however, goes beyond that because it has to do with comprehending the actions and intentions of the other person. In other words, it means putting yourself in the other person's place, or walking in his shoes. It is a kind of inference in which observation, memory, knowledge, and reasoning are combined to understand the thoughts and feelings of others. In the field of neuroscience, there is already talk of empathy neurons, or mirror neurons, which are involved in the understanding of other people's emotions. In fact, nowadays it is believed that in cases of autism, the mirror or empathy neurons are being blocked.

> **People can tell when you are trying to win their approval, or when you are merely acting in a hypocritical manner**

We become empathetic to the extent we take care in approaching others.

There are sales that are better not to make at certain

times. For example, if the person is irritable or in a bad mood, it is better not to bring up the subject but to leave the sale for another time. You could endear yourself to that person, without directly mentioning the sale, and only identifying with what happened in that moment —which will make you empathetic.

I remember an incident that occurred a few years ago as I was visiting a gentleman. As soon as I was about to bring up the subject of a sale, something happened at his house. He received a phone call informing him about the situation, so I put aside the reason for my visit. We got in my car, and I drove him home so he could resolve his problem; I gave him all the help I could. Afterward, I said goodbye, and we both agreed to speak again another time. Sure enough, two weeks later, we were talking business. I closed the sale, and he became one of my best customers. With time, we became good friends; so much so, that we still keep in touch today.

When you empathize, you should not try to clown around; neither should you be a hypocrite. Empathy is like a somersault: as you dive into it, you can do it the best you can, or you can die in the attempt. People can tell when you are trying to win their approval, or when you are merely acting in a hypocritical manner. You must be mindful of this and take care what you say or do. Ask yourself: Am I capable of empathizing?

THE EMPATHY THAT BLUNDERS

One time there was a man standing on the side of a road, and another gentleman stopped his vehicle to give him a ride. He offered to take the rider close to his destination. During the ride, the passenger didn't know how to reach out to the driver who had done him the favor, since he was very silent and serious. In fact, the driver was so serious that his passenger didn't speak at all, because he didn't want to offend him.

◇◇◇◇◇◇◇◇◇◇◇◇◇◇◇◇◇◇◇◇◇◇◇◇

A good salesperson must be a good observer

◇◇◇◇◇◇◇◇◇◇◇◇◇◇◇◇◇◇◇◇◇◇◇◇

The rider thought to himself, What if I talk about the Yankees, and he turns out to be a Boston fan? And what if I bring up the Republicans, and he's a Democrat? He kept wondering if he should talk about this, that, or the other thing. Then the passenger said, "Well, yes … ," to which the driver answered, "Well, no! Get out of my car right now." One simple phrase made this man have to step out of the vehicle.

This story is a joke, but the idea is that you must choose your words carefully when attempting to empathize. To connect, you should be trying to reach out to others before even contacting them. Find out what your customers do for a living. What do they like to do for fun? Are they married? Do they have children? How many? Do they like golf or baseball? What sports teams do they support? If you already know someone enjoys golf, stop by a golf shop to get a small souvenir, and say, "I'll stop by your office to bring you a small present because I know you like golf." By doing this, you are showing empathy because you are expressing interest in something your customer likes. This will later become something through which you can reach out to them. Of course, you must be prudent and respect the privacy of people, which I have already discussed.

There are salespeople who arrive to visit their customers in a hurry, and notice a painting hanging on the wall and start to talk about that painting. Sometimes that may work, but 80 percent of the time, it results in nothing. First, you must understand that the people who reach certain positions or establish businesses are smart, regardless of how unassuming they may seem to be. Therefore, when you try to empathize, keep in mind you are dealing with a human being with a high level of intelligence. If you try to empathize on the basis of hypocrisy, it is likely he will notice and lose confidence in you. So if the moment is not right, avoid thinking about the subject of sales.

A good salesperson must be a good observer.

Observe how the desks and offices are arranged. When you sit in the waiting room, look carefully at every detail. If you have the opportunity to do so, observe how your customer speaks to his own staff and customers. Using these visual and auditory clues, you will find out what kind of person is inside that office. This will help you, when you enter through that door, to empathize more specifically with that person. Keep your eyes open. If you notice the customer's desk

◇◇◇◇◇◇◇◇◇◇◇◇◇◇◇◇◇◇◇◇◇◇◇◇◇◇◇◇◇◇

Every person you approach will react in a distinct manner How to empathize depends greatly on temperament

◇◇◇◇◇◇◇◇◇◇◇◇◇◇◇◇◇◇◇◇◇◇◇◇◇◇◇◇◇◇

is well organized, you will know you are dealing with a meticulous, organized person; if it is unorganized, or half organized, these are also signs. Also, finding a couch instead of a desk is a signal because every detail of a place has meaning.

If you wish to be able to empathize, open up your senses. Pay attention to what you have in front of you. No two customers are alike; therefore, you must adapt yourself to the time, place, and person you wish to win over. Listen to every message and pay attention, being respectful of the silent spaces. Listening is more important than speaking. Although technical knowledge of your products is highly important, you should not talk the ears off your customer. Many salespeople are unable to empathize because they don't know how to listen.

KNOWING THE TEMPERAMENTS

Every person you approach will react in a distinct manner. How to empathize depends greatly on temperament. There are four basic types of temperaments. Hippocrates divided these temperaments into the sanguine, the choleric, the phlegmatic, and the melancholic.

I recommend studying this point in depth. Find a book that deals with this topic; research the temperaments because I won't be explaining all about them here. I do want you to know that every temperament must be approached in a different manner. Interacting with a sanguine personality (someone spontaneous, emotional, warm, and talkative) is not the same as dealing with a melancholic person, (someone quiet, calm, calculating, and critical, with a roller-coaster aspect to his emotions and somewhat complex). The level of proof and details that a melancholic person requires differs from that of a sanguine person. You have to know how to get around a sanguine person because it is easy for him or her to derail you from your objective by talking so much.

Choleric people are more direct; they get straight to the point. For these individuals, it is easier to talk prices and results, although they may sometimes appear hostile or detached. But if you establish something in common with them, they will become your best customers. Phlegmatic people are usually detail-oriented, quieter, calmer, less talkative, and more careful; they normally think a lot before making a decision because they are very analytical.

All of these characteristics make it necessary to approach people in a different manner so that the process of winning their confidence and showing empathy will go along with what they like, with what makes them feel comfortable. If you are able to find the correct approach, the customer will feel confidence in you as a representative, a salesman, an executive, an adviser, an upline.

If the person you are approaching is a referral, speak with whoever referred him to you and ask for certain information: Is the referral talkative or quiet? How does he get along with others? How does he communicate? There is no point asking what kind of temperament he has because not everyone knows that kind of detail. But with a few simple questions, you will have an idea of the type of person he is, and you'll have the resources to help you empathize. Remember that empathizing is essential for winning the trust of your customers, and winning their trust is an essential part of being able to establish a long-term relationship with them.

So far, we have been discussing some aspects of the subject of confidence. The first is what you feel inside of you: "for out of the abundance of the heart the mouth speaks." The second is how you look, how you project yourself physically. The third has to do with the tools and materials you need to possess. The fourth deals with what you say: the words you use and the knowledge you have about the product you are offering. And the fifth aspect is empathy and the influence of the various temperaments in achieving empathy. Next, I will discuss the sixth and final point necessary to winning true confidence.

6. CONFIDENCE PUT TO THE TEST: LIFE OR DEATH

Over twenty years ago, a famous American pharmaceutical company suffered from an act of sabotage. It discovered that many of the bottles of one of its most popular analgesics contained pills with cyanide. Some people ingested these contaminated pills, and several poisoning deaths resulted throughout the United States. What did the company do when they discovered that some of their pill bottles contained cyanide? They had two options available: leave everything up in the air and cast the blame on a third party, or face the problem responsibly. The company decided to recall the products that had been distributed worldwide; it stopped advertising and halted all sales. Millions of pill bottles were recalled and billions of dollars lost. The company had to regroup, make a new product, and work to win back the consumers' confidence. During the crisis, this pharmaceutical outfit made no profit and lost a great deal of money. In the end, however, it retained something very important that allowed it to stay in the market and keep its leading position: the confidence of its customers.

> **If a company, an individual, a church, or any other institution loses the confidence of the people, it will have lost everything**

If a company, an individual, a church, or any other institution loses the confidence of the people, it will have lost everything.

People do not want to go to a place or associate with those they do not trust. I have dedicated all this time and space to this subject so you understand how important it is to see in yourself a trustworthy person when you look in the mirror.

It is important that when you give someone your word, you do what you promised; that when you say you'll be there at a certain hour, you arrive on time; that when you empathize, you do so in a sincere manner; because all of the signals that you give will demonstrate whether you are a trustworthy individual or someone who cannot be trusted.

I encourage you to be a trustworthy person today and always, because this is the first tool for becoming a successful salesperson.

CHAPTER TWO

IN-DEPTH ANALYSIS

Questions are the master key to negotiations.

The second step, pillar, or column of a successful sale is the in-depth analysis. I'm going to ask you to take a few seconds to carefully repeat these words aloud: *in-depth analysis.*

Imagine that you are going to see a doctor. As soon as you enter his office, before even sitting down, the doctor prescribes you some medicine and then asks you to come back in a few days for an operation. My question to you is, would you place yourself in the hands of this doctor? It would be impossible for any health professional to tell you that you need of surgery without having first talked with you and examined you. Under what circumstances would you agree to that operation?

Sometimes the same thing happens with salespeople. Before they even take a seat in their customers' offices, they are already telling them what they need.

Customers do not buy what you offer them; they buy what they really need.

It is true that some individuals don't know what they need. But for the most part, when people go out to buy something, they generally have a good idea what they are going to buy, even though they may not show it. Remember: the customer must be treated as an intelligent human being because that is what he is.

A few days ago, I called a mechanic to inspect the air conditioning in my vehicle. We agreed to meet in the parking lot of a radio station where I produce a program. Upon arriving, I left a friend with the mechanic while I went inside. As soon as I entered the broadcast booth, my friend sent a text message to my cell phone: "Come down. The mechanic says the repairs will cost forty thousand pesos" (the equivalent of US$1,000). The truth is, I did not understand how he had decided on that figure since he hadn't even inspected the car yet! The mechanic just opened the hood and said this, that, or the other needed to be replaced, and the repairs would cost that amount of money. We're talking about a car that was practically new!

There are people who always try to take others by surprise without understanding that most human beings are intelligent. Regardless of their academic level or whether they attended school, their common sense and life experiences have made them intelligent. So never trust a person who has not given you an in-depth analysis of the situation. Likewise, a successful salesperson must be thorough; he must ask the right questions (at the right time), take good notes, and think about what he will say to show interest in the customer.

A good salesperson does not distinguish himself only by what he says but also by the questions he asks. Why make an in-depth analysis? First, a salesperson who immediately makes recommendations off the cuff can insult the customer because he is not showing respect for the customer's level of intelligence. Even though the customer may need what the salesperson is offering,

> **Remember: the customer must be treated as an intelligent human being because that is what he is**

he may resist the sale. If you do this when you go out to sell, you are likely to lose sales and long-term relationships. You will lose contact with the customer because you didn't take your time to make the appropriate analysis before starting to make offers. Second, making a good sale is impossible if you don't know what the other person needs. You may say, "Well, the gentleman said he needed a car, and that's what I'm doing: selling a car." But what if the car is not for him but for his wife, daughter, or mother-in-law? There may be hundreds of potential owners for a car, and each one corresponds to a certain kind of demographic. A car meant for the owner of a business is not the same as the car meant for a manager or employee; a car meant for someone's wife is not the same as a car meant for another family member. Even though each person may say they wish to buy a product, inside they may have a thousand different reasons why they wish to buy it. You cannot make a good sale without knowing what the customer wants.

If you don't ask the right questions or make an in-depth analysis, you won't discover the real needs of the customer.

Many people say they are creating a need. But we have absolutely no business whatsoever creating a need for anyone, in the first place, nor is it an ethical thing to do, in the second place. I cannot go to your home to make you see that you need a washing machine when you really have no need for one.

SEARCHING FOR REAL NEEDS

A "good analysis" suggests that you and your customer will find out what his or her real needs are at that moment and how these can be satisfied with a product you are selling. People know what their needs are;

therefore, the salesperson should become a coach or adviser so the customer may get the product that best suits their needs. The salesperson is a conductor or a consultant; by means of an in-depth analysis, he helps the customer to see, recognize, and understand his need by bringing it to light. He does not create the need; he discovers it. They both work together to supply the demand for something that perhaps

If you don't ask the right questions or make an in-depth analysis, you won't discover the real needs of the customer

the customer has not contemplated but really is in need of. This is better than creating a need. When you create a need, the customer may buy something due to feeling pressured or confused, but later he may come to curse the sale or the salesperson. You might say, "What does it matter if he curses me? I've already made the sale!" Well, in that case, I would tell you: it matters. If you have one hundred customers and all one hundred of them speak poorly of you and discredit you, you will become a salesperson with a bad reputation. And as everyone knows, it is incredibly difficult to live down a bad reputation.

Regardless of what your beliefs may be, I must tell you

that spiritually, cursing has a very negative influence on people's lives. Personally, I wouldn't want even one single person cursing me because they have a product in their house they shouldn't have bought; and now every time they see it, they think of me, and wish to blow it up in my face. In summary, ill will, a tarnished reputation, and curses are just some of the things that can be reaped if you go around the world creating needs in order to sell things to people that they don't need.

◇◇◇◇◇◇◇◇◇◇◇◇◇◇◇◇◇◇◇◇◇◇◇◇◇◇
The majority of customers prefer dealing with just one sales executive to supply all their requirements
◇◇◇◇◇◇◇◇◇◇◇◇◇◇◇◇◇◇◇◇◇◇◇◇◇◇

Another important reason to carry out an in-depth analysis is to achieve a more fulfilling, comprehensive and complete sale. For example, suppose your catalog contains ten products, but you are focused on selling quickly; with any luck you may be able to sell one— even though it is likely your customer may need five of them. He may even need all ten, but since you did not carry out an in-depth analysis of the situation, your vision was limited by your rush to sell. An in-depth analysis means that you care about the real needs of your customer. You have ten products in your catalog, and if you start to converse, ask questions, and insert yourself into your customer's thinking processes (being respectful of his boundaries), you will surely be able to meet many of his demands with the products you are offering. However, if you don't ask questions, observe, inquire or analyze the situation, instead of selling $10,000 worth of products, you will only sell $500; and another more intelligent salesperson may come and make the other $9,500 worth of sales.

The majority of customers prefer dealing with just one sales executive to supply all their requirements. You should be the one to win their confidence so they will choose you.

In that sense, an in-depth analysis is very helpful because the customer won't have to turn to so many different people, something that costs time and money; and the salesperson can sell a greater quantity of products to a single customer. Think about this: a salesperson would not have to go from customer to customer to meet his goal of $10,000 in sales; he could reach it by selling to a single customer frankly in need. Always remember: a salesperson is considered good or successful not on the basis of how much he says, but the questions he asks. When you have worked up a battery of interesting questions, the customer will feel more comfortable and confident.

When people go to see a doctor, they are generally suffering from one of two types of problems: physical or psychological. It often happens that an individual can feel sick, believe he is indeed sick, and go to see the doctor to discuss his illness and analyze certain symptoms. However, the doctor may conclude that the patient is not physically ill but is overloaded and suffering from stress; he leaves the office, trusting what the doctor has told him. In two days' time, he will feel completely well, without having taken a single pill. This means there was a great deal of psychological pressure, but despite the fact that the individual was sure his health was in bad shape, once he talked with his doctor, he discovered that many aspects of his life could produce an emotional burden and make him feel sick. The same thing happens when a sales executive helps a customer. Apart from making sales, you become a coach, someone your customer has to trust; you end up becoming a great friend. You will sell, and he will buy; there is no doubt about that. But so much well-being was received in the process of negotiation that the customer will decide to keep you around as his adviser.

◇◇◇◇◇◇◇◇◇◇◇◇◇◇◇◇◇◇◇◇◇◇◇◇◇◇◇◇
Questions are the master key for every salesperson
◇◇◇◇◇◇◇◇◇◇◇◇◇◇◇◇◇◇◇◇◇◇◇◇◇◇◇◇

These are not the things that can be gotten from any

ordinary person. These things can be gotten from sales executives and vendors who have carried out an in-depth analysis, and who have studied the structure of a sale in a scientific manner, if you will.

HOW TO PERFORM AN IN-DEPTH ANALYSIS

To carry out an in-depth analysis, it is necessary to come up with a series of questions. Every industry has its own fundamentals on which its products are based. If you sell electrical equipment or appliances, there are questions about electricity. If you sell bottled water, there are questions about the water industry. If you are in the multilevel marketing business, you should think about what questions to ask to sponsor someone. A life insurance agent should find out how old a customer is, what his occupation is, how many children he has, the ages of his children, and so on. These are the kinds of questions that will determine how much the customer will spend on that insurance policy. The value of the policy will have a great deal to do with the relationship between the customer's age and the value being insured, the number of children, and their incomes. Regardless of what you sell, there are certain questions you should have ready before you go out into the street. You should have an idea of what you need to know about the customer to be able to close the deal.

"I seriously doubt anyone could sell me a product without knowing how to ask me the right questions."

Questions are the master key for every salesperson. First, remember that you must know your industry and its fundamental questions well before approaching the customer. Second, you should learn everything there is to know about the company you represent so that you can answer correctly any questions your customer might have. Knowing your company is important because the more you know about it, the easier it will be to disarm any objections the customer may raise about past experiences with similar companies or products. This knowledge will serve as backup and will become a great strength that will allow you to clear up any doubts that might come up during a sale.

As a salesperson, you should also learn everything you can about the product and how people normally solve their problems that may arise with it. Let me explain. As a vitamin or supplements salesperson, you should know everything there is to know about the healthcare industry. You should know how people solve problems in that area. You should also be able to recognize the mood your customer is in. Find out whether your customer has been sick; ask questions that will give you clues as to how things are going with your customer's health. This will allow you a more assertive strategy based on the products you are offering. If you recommend products only because they are good or for this or that reason, you may end up leaving without selling anything. Perhaps the customer is suffering from acid stomach; but since you didn't carry out an in-depth investigation, and you didn't show any interest in his health or life, and all you could come up with was recommending pills, the customer will end up telling you he isn't interested in buying. (He won't even tell you why he didn't buy anything, because they generally never do.) Everything will come to a halt because you trusted in your ability to sell what you wanted to sell and not what the customer wanted to buy. When carrying out an in-depth analysis, you have to understand that the customer has his own reasons for buying a product. I hope you never forget that.

The third point about how to perform an in-depth analysis is exactly this: finding the reasons in the hearts and minds of your customers.

Regardless of what a customer may be looking to buy —from rockets to light bulbs, he will have his own reasons for doing so.

REASONS FOR BUYING: THE CONCEPT

The reason a customer has for buying something is

what is known as a concept; and in this sense, the word concept refers to the significance a customer gives to a certain product. What does your product mean to the customer? For example, a gentleman walks into a shoe store and asks for a pair of shoes. The salesperson takes the man to another area and starts to bring out shoes for him to try. Here is where the ritual begins: Salesperson brings out a pair of shoes; gentleman tries them on. Salesperson brings out another pair; gentleman tries them on. Then another pair.... Finally, the salesperson asks the customer, "Do you like these? Did you like those? Are they comfortable?"

But the annoyed customer stands up and says, "I don't want any of them."

"But sir, what's wrong? You didn't like those?" asks the salesclerk. "Look, we have another pair on sale today right over here."

"But I don't need a pair of shoes for myself," says the customer. "What I need is a pair of shoes for my wife."

This is what is referred to as the concept. The concept for that gentleman, in that moment, was not shoes for himself but shoes for his wife. The first thing the salesclerk should have done was determine for whom he planned to buy shoes. The salesperson could have asked other appropriate questions: What's the occasion? What size does she wear? Would she like high heels or flats? Are you looking for any color in particular? Finding out why a customer wants to buy applies not only to direct sales in stores but also to sales carried out by independent sellers.

The seller needs to discover the customer's concept, whether the customer came of his own accord or was approached by the seller.

In the case of the shoe salesman, it was a simple matter. Many sales associates employed in stores make the same mistake time and time again. Some of them follow the customer around like guards, saying things like, "If you need something, let me know" or "We're here if you need any help." Many salespeople take for granted that when customers wish to buy something, they are shopping only for themselves. These sellers have formed preconceived notions of the reasons why a customer has to buy, and they think the customer's reasons are in sync with their own understanding. So, when you carry out an in-depth analysis, you are discovering the concept. I could give

> **So, when you carry out an in-depth analysis, you are discovering the concept**

innumerable examples, like the case of car dealerships. The concept of a classic vehicle is not the same as that of a family car, regardless of how much better, newer, or more affordable it may be.

Martha, one of my wife's friends, sells clothing and handbags for women. When it is time for her to stock up with new merchandise, she thinks about every single one of her customers. She knows her clientele: what each one's occupation is; which ones are executives and which ones are more sports-minded; how each one generally spends her free time. She knows the women's sizes, what colors they find most attractive, and what their husbands do for a living. By the time she returns from a buying trip, she has her new merchandise practically sold, because her next step is calling her customers and saying, "Dear, I got something especially for you. Come and see it." Not only that, but she also observes their daughters; she knows their ages and the kind of clothing they generally wear, so that the ladies will also take something home for the younger ones of the house. This friend of ours has done an in-depth analysis of each one of her customers and knows their concepts, which is why she almost never has unsold merchandise. She knows she can't afford the luxury of having it lying around. This woman does not buy merchandise for her business just because it looks pretty; she buys it because it meets the precise needs of her clientele in a timely way.

Regardless of what the customer may be looking to buy, from rockets to light bulbs, he will have his own reasons for doing so. The in-depth analysis aims to insert itself into the mind of the prospect to discover his fundamental reason for wanting a certain product, or why he ought to have it, from his perspective. If the customer does not know that perspective, it is the seller's responsibility to help him discover it correctly, and not impose it on him.

FOUR AREAS OF ESSENTIAL QUESTIONS

Apart from the battery of questions used to carry out an analysis, there are four types of essential questions that a seller should typically ask. We are looking at generalities, since not all products are alike, and different industries call for different questions.

There are questions that are exclusive to one type of industry or trade.

Some questions can be ignored due to time constraints. You do not have the same time for questions when selling a pair of shoes in a store as you would when selling an insurance policy or signing someone up for a multilevel marketing company. Every area, opportunity, and contact has questions that will have differing levels of depth to them; some will be more lightweight than others. But the important thing is making the correct analysis.

1. PEOPLE'S FEELINGS

The first area of questions has to do with people's feelings. Regardless of whether you are trying to sell a candle or a military tank, it is important that the person you have in front of you knows you are interested in how they are doing. You should ask things like, "How are you feeling?" "How are you today?" You should add phrases such as, "It's a pleasure to meet you"; "It's good to see you," and "It's a great opportunity to meet today!" You are speaking with another human being who has feelings, not with a machine. Even something as simple as a hurting fingernail can change the way a person reacts, which can affect a negotiation. That is why it is so important to recognize other people's moods; listen to what they are saying through their words, their gestures, and their faces. The face can say quite

> **If you don't capture the attention of a customer, you will accomplish nothing**

a bit. Even though it is not always wise to judge by appearances, generally in sales, an uncomfortable face says something.

As I have covered previously, people's temperaments will influence how open or closed they will be. The skill of a salesperson lies in being able to define the customer through a series of simple questions that will later become a master key that will open the possibility of closing a sale. This is another reason it is important to take your time. As a question is being asked and answered, it is marking the path for the next question; one question leads to another. It is through a series of questions that you can reach a deeper understanding.

In years past, the AIDA method was commonly used in marketing. AIDA is an acronym for the words **attention**, **interest**, **desire**, and **action**. If you don't capture the attention of

> **The first area of questions has to do with people's feelings**

a customer, you will accomplish nothing. Therefore, it is of utmost importance to visualize the human being in front of you; get rid of any unrelated thoughts that may be in your mind and may prevent you from capturing the customer's undivided attention. These questions pertaining to human character have no direct relation to the sale itself. However, they can open a door through which it is possible to obtain the attention you need them to give you. Perhaps the conversation may end there; questions of this type are not always guaranteed to close a deal since the answers will determine if it's possible to continue talking. For example, a person may reply, "I am feeling devastated at this moment because I have just lost a family member," or "I'm feeling quite tired. Now is not a good time to buy." In cases such as these, obviously you should not force a sale. At least you will have made good use of that time and established contact. In any event, it is very important that when you go out to sell, you think not only about what you can get, but put the human aspect first and identify how you can be of help, of comfort or simply give people the space they need at that moment.

2. THE CUSTOMER'S VISION

Every time I was tasked with visiting an important customer, I focused on finding out what his vision for his business was: where did he see himself in the long term? It is very difficult to help someone who lacks a defined vision. By asking a customer about his vision, you are aiming to find out if what you are offering has any relevance to what he is imagining he will accomplish in future years; but also, you can find ways to make a contribution to his life. Sometimes you want to help someone in regard to their future who may be very sure of what they are pursuing (something that often happens in intangible businesses); however, there are others who are so disoriented regarding their future, they are like ships lost at sea with a likelihood of sinking.

◇◇◇◇◇◇◇◇◇◇◇◇◇◇◇◇◇◇◇◇◇◇◇

By delving into their vision, you can tell if it is more beneficial to help them out of their present condition or leave them where they are

◇◇◇◇◇◇◇◇◇◇◇◇◇◇◇◇◇◇◇◇◇◇◇

By delving into their vision, you can tell if it is more beneficial to help them out of their present condition or leave them where they are.

Whether or not you can help depends on the cost that one alternative or the other may involve. There are people whose vision is buried so deep that it is better not to do any kind of business with them; there is little chance of satisfying their needs, for they are far removed from what you are thinking. On the other hand, there are many individuals who are really clear about what it is they are after, and it would be wise to see if any of it is in tune with what you can offer them.

Asking customers about what they do in their businesses or where they see themselves going will give you a much broader idea of the needs you could be fulfilling, whether they are tangible or intangible, in the present or in the future.

You should find out how or where the customer sees himself or his business: Is he thinking about moving or expanding the store? Does he have competition across the street? If the business is a retail outlet, is he looking to become a wholesale vendor? If he currently sells underwear, is he looking to introduce other types of products? Is his vision to be the number one store in the city? Every aspect of a vision brings a different need. The vision of a person, a business or a company, largely defines their present and future needs. The question, where do you see yourself, is what determines whether you can contribute to satisfying those needs.

In multilevel marketing systems, when one person tries to sponsor another but doesn't know where his prospect sees himself in the next few years, the sponsor will have a hard time helping the prospect obtain favorable results. Imagine a business consultant trying to sponsor someone who likes everything related to the arts and has already positioned himself in that line of work. The consultant motivates him to become a better businessman, to make more money, and to dream more about what he, the consultant, is thinking, rather than what the prospect wishes to achieve. It is possible that this person's vision for the next ten years is to become a great movie star or singer; and since people are influenced by personal interests and tastes, from my perspective, it will be quite difficult for him to focus on another type of activity. The business consultant must be very careful when it comes to trying to inject his own vision. It is not enough to simply say that what he is offering is better because it will allow his candidate to make more money and will open up more opportunities for him. The sponsor may even say, "You'll be able to achieve your dream in art once you have more money." They forget that quite likely the person already has a well-defined goal. Unfortunately, in many of these cases, the prospects are left with a bad taste in their mouths regarding the activity they are being introduced to, driving them away forever. Not only that, but think of the time that was lost that could have been used with another person.

An individual who is linked to the arts does not necessarily relate well with money but rather with fame or the simple act of being "spontaneous," as he might say. So what ends up happening is that he is not in tune with what his consultant is offering him.

Clearly I am not saying it is impossible. What I am saying is that in cases like these, changing a life that is already clear about and on its way toward what it is pursuing and its future will take more time, patience, and dedication. It will require an all-out effort to understand the individual's thought processes and vision in order to find a point of common interest. The adviser must do his utmost to match the customer's vision to what he is offering. If I know the vision, I will know how to lead my customer toward it. If I know what my customer is looking for in his future, I will be able to find the right place for him in my portfolio, my products, and my organization because I will be on the right track.

If I know the vision, I will know how to lead my customer toward it

Identifying the vision correctly is not an easy matter. Asking the right questions about this aspect requires work and care. Regardless of how small my product may be, linking the customer's personal vision with his vision of what I offer can provide better opportunities. Question like: What do you really think about this? How do you envision yourself in regard to my proposal? Do you think it will provide you with good opportunities? In what ways do you think it will benefit you? will shed light on the concept and help you find the right place for your customer.

3. PAST EXPERIENCES

The third type of questions I like to ask have to do with people's past, especially their past as consumers. If you sell insurance, then it is essential to have the customer tell you what company has been insuring him for the past few years, what type of policy or coverage he has had, and who his agents have been, whether you know them or not. Experiences with agents, companies, services, or claims will give you many clues about what the customer is thinking.

The customer expresses his feelings on his face.

If the customer's past experiences were negative, that will be a good thing to know; it will help you avoid mentioning issues that bother him, companies that have failed him, products that did not meet his expectations, or plans that are not in line with his requirements. If it has to do with a service, past experiences are a fundamental point that may ruin the satisfaction you are trying to provide for him. If it's a tangible consumer product, it may offer a real benefit—unlike the product the customer believes is irrelevant to his interests.

Let's go back to the example of multilevel companies. I like using multilevel sales because I believe they offer a great deal of knowledge; it is a very interesting line of business that offers great opportunities. Let's suppose that you are trying to sponsor someone, and this person was previously affiliated with your own organization or perhaps another competing company.

> **Believe it or not, past experiences will become either your best friend or your worst enemy during a sale**

It is important to know the person's opinion about their past experiences because it will help you avoid making mistakes.

You don't need to find out the name if the same company is involved. But you should find out what the previous sponsor said or did that caused that person to leave the business. Obviously, this kind of information should be handled in an ethical, prudent, and respectful manner. You should know how much time has passed since the bad experience; it could be something from years ago that would have no bearing on the present or the way things are currently handled. Perhaps you may tell the person he'll become a millionaire in a certain amount of time; but that person has already gone through that experience before, and it did not happen the way they said it would. In summary, there are a great number of experiences in every aspect of life: marriage, family, goals, time, money, and products. All of these are involved in the experiences of the people who run a business; therefore, it's advisable to investigate and listen carefully so you can have a better idea of how it should be handled. Believe it or not, past experiences will become either your best friend or your worst enemy during a sale. The customer may say, "I already went through this

> **It is important to know the person's opinion about their past experiences because it will help you avoid making mistakes**

before"; or "They already told me that, and it didn't happen." You may have a different vision that can guide your prospect down the right path, one which truly offers them a good opportunity. You must be sure of it though; and you must be prepared to see that your new ideas have nothing to do with their bad experiences.

Another point to keep in mind is that when a customer

has had a bad experience, he almost never tells about it in the beginning. Unless it was something that really upset him and the experience has been very hurtful to him, it is very likely the person will keep quiet during their first meetings with you. The customer will begin to observe every detail in silence because he's comparing you with his previous adviser, or he's decoding every proposal you present with his past experiences. Remember we have told you that most people are not fools.

People are intelligent—they don't go around believing everything that is said to them.

Never try to outsmart anyone, because the customer is generally very observant, especially if it's a service. The sales of tangibles or consumer goods are more likely to create sporadic relationships that don't require as much mental effort. Selling a painting is not the same as selling an insurance policy. If you just happen to resemble a previous seller or middleman, and you remind the person of someone who tricked them or who made an offer that left them with a bitter experience, don't count on closing that sale. The person will keep quiet and simply say no—not because of who you are but because you remind him in some way of that other seller. He will think you are trying to do the same thing to him that the previous one did. The best thing to do is give the prospect time, so that in subsequent encounters he can begin to express those bitter emotions and tell you what he considers to be harmful about the industry, the product, or the company you represent. The customer might be confused and the product isn't even yours. But then again, it might be yours; and you are caught red-handed trying to sell a product that had already been offered and which that particular customer has had a very bad experience with. What good will that do? If you know the history, you may be able to make a difference between one product and another, which many times has to do with the person who provides it. You can appeal to the fact that you will be different, and you will not cheat him. Perhaps that experience is not the common denominator and you can prove it. You can say, "Hundreds of people have used this product. Nevertheless, I can tell you how it should be used. I know the correct proportions and how to combine them. I am very familiar with the service I am offering. The products are the same because they are made in the same plant. But I can assure you that with the kind of consulting you will receive from me, your experience will be completely satisfactory."

What difference is there between two products made with the same components, in the same factory, and having the same name? None. The only difference is

> **Even though the product may be the same, the vendor makes the difference with his service**

the vendor's service. Even though the product may be the same, the vendor makes the difference with his service. If he knows the product well and how to use it, and does the job correctly, he will profit greatly from offering good service. For example, a medical equipment sales representative has in his portfolio a number of instruments and machines. He may meet with a client that has had a very bad experience. Perhaps the supplier is not one of the most well-known, or the sales representatives company is small and has the reputation of not delivering orders on time. Nonetheless, the sales representative can make the most remarkable difference. To the extent that he follows up and gives good service, he will change the perception of those products and that company.

I like companies that teach their executives the importance of customer service and how they can meet their sales objectives according to how much effort and good service they are able to offer. The product may be the same, but the sales representative's service is different. When you know what you're doing, when you know the customer has had bitter experiences, you can then rely on your qualities as a consultant. You will be selling yourself; that's why it's so essential to be well-informed about all of your customer's experiences. In addition, if the customer has had any good experiences in his previous sales relationships, satisfying him will be a greater challenge. If a customer has bought something at a better price, it is not possible for you to sell it to him at a higher price. If this situation were to arise, the customer would keep quiet and say, "I'd rather buy from the other guy at a better price." This could label you as someone who tries to take advantage of consumers. And believe me: rumors spread like wildfire in the world of sales.

If you investigate their past experiences, this will help you to be on the alert. And if you offer your product for a little higher price, at least then you have that

◇◇◇◇◇◇◇◇◇◇◇◇◇◇◇◇◇◇◇◇◇◇◇◇◇◇◇◇◇

I like companies that teach their executives the importance of customer service...

◇◇◇◇◇◇◇◇◇◇◇◇◇◇◇◇◇◇◇◇◇◇◇◇◇◇◇◇◇

extra something to justify the higher price; you will have a valid explanation for the difference in price. It may be justified on the basis of your advice, your follow-up, issues of time, an added value of the product, a changing rate, or another component of the product. There may be a thousand reasons why the value of a product may vary, but you should stay ahead of the curve with valid arguments to respond to the customer's questions.

4. THE NEED FOR THE PRODUCT

Lastly, we have the type of questions regarding the need for the product. Even though I have already covered this somewhat, I would like to analyze it further. Let's use the shoe store as an example again. The customer enters a store, and the salesperson asks his first questions: "How are you today?" "How may I help you?" "Have you been to this store before or to one of our other locations?" Based on the answer, he asks the customer what his experience was like. "Were you pleased with the price?" The salesperson then finds out from the customer about his vision for the shoes—this is vital for determining what type of shoes he's looking for—and whether he's buying for himself or another person. The salesperson can be asking the questions quickly while the customer browses through the store; this allows him to eliminate options and save time. He can find out more about the occasion: are the shoes for a party? a graduation? work? school? the beach? any specific color? If the customer answers, "Any color will do," then they will have to go through the different color options in the store. The salesperson can take the opportunity to ask, "Are you going to match them with something special?" This question may guide her toward finding the right color shoes, especially if the customer is a woman. If the salesperson can guide the customer into telling him whether she would prefer laced shoes or slippers, round toes or pointed, the salesperson will have more opportunities to narrow down the options between the thousands of models that are found in stores. This will allow him to be assertive, as customers generally do not enjoy being shown shoes at random if they already have a clear idea of what they are looking for. Personally, that is something that irritates and exasperates me as well, to be quite honest. Doing this will make life easier not only for the salesperson but also for the customer. In cases like these, it helps to make key questions short and concise. Businesses like shoe stores and supermarkets operate on limited time, so clerks should be as precise as possible.

With these questions about the need for the product, the salesperson will have a brief but accurate reference about the customer that may be used to evaluate him or her. If the customer answers that he has not shopped at this store before, the salesperson will have a great opportunity.

Formerly, in the 1980s and 1990s, many families had a preferred shoe store where they did their shopping. I remember that whenever my parents thought about buying shoes, they already had a store in mind, and that was where they went first. In fact, they always asked for the same salesman, whom they greeted by name and who made them feel important and respected. Nowadays, we are in an age of instant results, so you have to learn to be proactive and use your time efficiently.

Creating a more complete profile of a prospective customer will allow you to land a more certain offer.

Now let's look at the example of multilevel companies, which are more complex. To ascertain the needs of a prospect, a multilevel adviser may inquire about physical or economic matters in a subtle manner; he may ask questions related to the prospect's health, average income, dreams, or goals. The adviser may also carry out an analysis of a prospect's income to find out how much money he has at the end of the month, how much of that is saved, and if the prospect has debts or credit cards. Many advisers use forms to answer questions about more complicated questions like these in an appointment, which gives them formality and professionalism, and avoids giving the impression that they are merely salespeople who just want to pry into the prospects' personal lives. When telling about the multilevel industry, the adviser should have a more complete profile of the individual

Creating a more complete profile of a prospective customer will allow you to land a more certain offer

seated in front of him: marital status, age, number of children, occupation, unfulfilled dreams or goals, where he sees himself in the next ten years. The adviser can then determine if he is dealing with a future downline or merely a consumer.

In the insurance business, it is important to know the extent of the customer's business investments: Does he have branch offices? If so, how many? Where are they located? Does he have a family (married or with children)? Does he have other properties, vehicles, or collateral businesses of a different nature? In many cases, a customer may have businesses in different industries; and if the seller concentrates on just one of them, he will miss opportunities to insure all the customer's properties or his family for health, life, accidents, or school insurance. Regardless of which trade, industry or organization your customer belongs to, never forget to ask if your customer is linked to any other type of business, because this will open great opportunities for you.

There are hundreds of questions that can be asked, and I want to encourage you to let your ability to ask questions go to work for you. These questions will help you expand the world of things you offer to your customers, have better aim in presenting your products, and grasp possible options to close deals.

When you ask a question, you turn on a light in the midst of the darkness

When you ask a question, you turn on a light in the midst of the darkness. I don't understand why there are people who insist on showing a product in the dark. When someone enters a room that has been closed, the intelligent thing to do is turn on the light, because it will be easier to see everything more clearly. When you ask key questions, you illuminate your mind, and your actions become more definite. Likewise, you know what to offer and what your customer needs. You are able to make an impact on people by illuminating their lives, and in many cases, their future. That's why questions are the most important tool a seller or adviser can develop.

If someone were to ask, what is the most common mistake made by salespeople? I would answer them with total certainty: not asking questions.

Not asking questions is a huge mistake because it means taking for granted that all your presuppositions apply to the life of the customer you have in front of you.

TAKE NOTES

When I started working as a salesman, I was advised

to carry a notebook to write down everything the customer told me. But like all beginners, I wanted to do things my way, make my own mistakes, and forge my own path. This is the worst mistake anyone can make, because the truth is, every mistake has already been made by hundreds and thousands of people who can share their experiences with us.

"Listen to advice and accept discipline, and at the end you will be counted among the wise." (Proverbs 19:20 NIV)

If you avoid making many of the mistakes others have already made, you can spare yourself many inconveniences and setbacks. So when someone says something to you, it is important to bear it in mind because it may be something that can help you save time. The roads have already been made; there are already avenues, airports, and highways you can travel on. Why invent another? I'm not telling you to stop being original or stop leaving your mark. What I am trying to communicate is that you should learn to accept advice. If your supervisor, upline, manager, or friend with sales experience suggests something to you, pay attention. If they recommend that you take notes, then take notes. If they tell you to record, take pictures, or research something in particular, then do so, while trying to understand what's behind it, what the other person learned by what they recommend, so you can learn, too. In that way, you may have a more direct path to success with fewer missteps.

When it comes to performing an in-depth analysis, taking notes is advantageous. I enjoy taking notes, and unfortunately, it is something I began to understand after my first experiences. I try to carry a camera, a recorder, or any other tool or object that can help me obtain the complete picture.

◇◇◇◇◇◇◇◇◇◇◇◇◇◇◇◇◇◇◇◇◇◇◇◇◇◇◇◇◇◇◇◇◇◇◇◇

When it comes to performing an in-depth analysis, taking notes is advantageous

◇◇◇◇◇◇◇◇◇◇◇◇◇◇◇◇◇◇◇◇◇◇◇◇◇◇◇◇◇◇◇◇◇◇◇◇

Before recording or taking pictures, you must ask permission and explain your reasons for doing so. Recording during the first meeting may feel awkward; you should be very clear so the customer clearly understands what the goal is. When you fail to take notes (or keep information), everything that was talked about is left in the mind, and as the saying goes, "the mind is treacherous." All of that valuable data may keep floating around, later to be forgotten, because, believe it or not, the mind is a fragile thing; it frequently forgets things. When taking notes, it is important to write clearly and orderly, so you understand them later. It's not about writing things at random but about asking questions, listening closely to the answers, and choosing the most relevant and important information; that is, filtering what is being communicated to you and noting key points or anything that may be a help to your analysis.

There are many people who jot down notes and end up not understanding any of what they have written. Use all of your senses (sight, touch, hearing, and sometimes even smell), since doing so will allow you to pay the utmost attention. Learn to take into account dates, locations, names given to you, sums or values, product or location specifications, number of members in a company or family. Never forget to write down something that a customer describes in detail. An intelligent customer will understand that someone who really is interested in learning something must take

When taking notes, it is important to write clearly and orderly, so you understand them later

notes. When you are seeing ten customers a day, it is impossible to retain all the information they have communicated. In my experience as vice president of sales, I discovered that a great number of salespeople and agents would tell customers, "I'm sorry, I forgot," which is very annoying. It is simply not possible for a salesperson or adviser who sees fifteen customers per week to remember everything. If you saw me on

Monday, another person on Tuesday, and another person every day, in a week and a half, you couldn't possibly remember everything I said on that Monday. Besides, the customer who sees the sales agent or adviser listening, supposedly, asking questions without taking any notes, the customer may become suspicious and think everything he tells him is going out into space and the salesperson is pulling his leg. I have already said customers are very intelligent.

Taking notes will allow you to review everything that customer has said and have the right facts available when preparing a proposal.

Many times while preparing an offer, after having trusted my memory and not taken notes, I realized I had forgotten or simply left out certain details. I embarrassingly had to call the customers to ask about something they had possibly already told me, thus wasting time and showing I was not an organized person. This caused me to lose many sales and deliver inaccurate presentations to those customers. Some of them even said to me, "But I already told you that," "That's not what I asked for," or "You forgot something." This is why I encourage you not to skip any detail, request, interest, or observation. You could fill several pages with details, but that's okay, because when you meet with your customer, you won't be making a speech or presentation to the wind. On the contrary, you will be taking something concrete and specific based on the perspective or vision the customer has already revealed, not on your own thoughts.

Another important reason for taking notes is the written record you can leave in case someone has to take your place. If you are sick, traveling, or being transferred, with these notes, someone can follow up on your work and have a more complete idea of what was discussed with the customer. There has been a case where a sales

Another important reason for taking notes is the written record you can leave in case someone has to take your place

agent or adviser has left a company after having quoted a price, and the one who came later quoted another price simply because there was nothing written down about the previous negotiations. Furthermore, these notes are evidence you visited the customers, followed up with them, and worked with them in depth. In areas like marketing, for example, sometimes there are sales forces where there is a great deal of internal competition. You may visit a customer and work very hard with them, only to have someone else assigned to that customer, whether by a manager's mistake or another reason. Without written notes, you would not be able to prove you had already been working with that customer.

This is why I always recommend, when salespeople go out to make a sale, whether they are selling an appliance, a piece of machinery, a photocopier, an insurance policy, or a hair product, that they try to provide a complete service

Another benefit of taking notes is that if you move to another firm in the same industry, your list of customers will stay with you because you know all the details about those customers; you know what to propose when you visit them with a new offer. The more extensive the notes you take, and the greater the level of details you have, the more effective and concrete your presentation will be. As a result, the customers will appreciate and value you more, cementing your relationships with them.

When I was an insurance salesman, whether I was presenting proposals on general risk or the branch of insurance for employees, I enjoyed going around the company (with its permission) taking pictures to look at them calmly and become acquainted with the organization more in depth. Doing this allowed me to get a good idea of how the structure of the company or the workforce was being managed, and it highlighted the importance of what that customer had built with his hands and effort. If I was dealing with the owner, he would feel appreciated, and assured that I was doing a serious job. What's more, by going around the place, I could check on things that the customer wouldn't notice, wouldn't tell me, or would forget to inform me about. This allowed me to discover insurance needs I would never have found had I been sitting at a desk. I could see areas where the customer needed to improve; I could make on-site observations regarding how to minimize risks, like where to place fire extinguishers and other technical matters. A simple observation could change the level of protection, safety or security of the company. This is why I always recommend, when salespeople go out to make a sale, whether they are selling an appliance, a piece of machinery, a photocopier, an insurance policy, or a hair product, that they try to provide a complete service.

Ask questions about the place, take notes, and go over the area. You should leave that place knowing how the business is run, how many people they receive, how much of a demand there is for their service, how their maintenance is. Don't sell something to companies or to people without first going around their place; in addition to safety, you could gain other customers. I love giving examples because you can learn from these experiences. Remember that others have already gone down this road, from which you should learn the best you can. If a car insurance agent goes out to sell a policy, it is advisable for him to ask permission to visit that customer's company. If the customer is the owner or manager, ideally the sales agent should try to walk around the facilities. The smart salesperson will sell not just one policy for a single vehicle but a policy to insure the entire fleet. He might also get to know the drivers in the transportation department and leave with future customers for his policies. He might inquire who is the head of Human Resources and work out a collective health or life insurance policy for the employees. If what he is selling is a cell phone and he visits his customer at his company, I can guarantee that the more he knows about his customer, the more his sales will increase.

◇◇◇◇◇◇◇◇◇◇◇◇◇◇◇◇◇◇◇◇◇◇◇◇◇◇◇◇◇

There is no deal too big for you to close

◇◇◇◇◇◇◇◇◇◇◇◇◇◇◇◇◇◇◇◇◇◇◇◇◇◇◇◇◇

I remember visiting a mining company whose insurance premium was over a million dollars. I was a young manager for an insurance company that wasn't exactly one of the biggest companies at the time. The firm had already signed a contract with another insurer, but I visited it anyway. Although the insured had been working with other brokers for several years, he confessed that he had never had such an in-depth conversation before, saying, "You do not always find people of this level of intelligence to talk to." To be honest, I was asking myself what kind of intelligence he was referring to; I was not a miner or an engineer, and I knew nothing about that activity. Why did that gentleman feel I was intelligent? Basically it was because I made him feel intelligent. I gave him an opportunity to talk about something he was interested in. I asked him detailed questions; I put on a hard hat and joined him on a tour of the mine to meet his managers and each one of his employees. This made him feel important and intelligent, since he was in his element as we chatted and he explained things. To

> **I gave him an opportunity to talk about something he was interested in**

my surprise, the company accepted my proposal and chose my insurance policy. Its account was transferred directly to the company because I was a manager, and the customer wanted me to manage its policies, which was a shame, because the broker could very well have kept that company's business.

There is no deal too big for you to close.

What am I trying to tell you with this? If you take the right steps, believe me, there is no deal too big for you to close. This implies that you should carry out an in-depth and detailed analysis, taking into account the high intelligence of your customers, their responsibilities (are they businesspeople? owners? executives? managers?), or if they have the money to buy. Remember that it is not possible for anyone who has made a great deal of money to lack intelligence, and I'm not talking about their academic level; I hope you bear this in mind. It is not logical for less wealthy salespeople to presume they are more intelligent than their customers, who have achieved much more. As a salesman, I can learn more things from my customers than they will from me. If you approach them with this attitude of learning, take into account their intelligence, and make them feel smart, I guarantee the next steps will be very simple; the sale will be practically a done deal. That is what it means to perform an in-depth analysis.

I wouldn't go in for surgery at the hands of a doctor who did not carry out a thorough diagnosis beforehand, who did not have lab tests or other special reports at hand, because my life would be at stake.

Although many might not believe it, a company in the hands of a sales consultant could put its future at risk.

The examples of this are many: Customers who insure themselves against fire, but when their businesses burn down, their claims are rejected because the insurance agents didn't do their jobs right; consumers who buy health insurance and are struck by a catastrophic illness, only to find that their policy does not cover it; machinery that doesn't do the job the customer thought it did, causing millions of dollars of losses; someone who invests thousands or millions of dollars in a business and does not manage to at least break even. You've seen it happen with the infamous pyramid schemes, and you see it happening daily in any area related to sales and business.

Before making an offer, know the details well so you can make accurate recommendations, present concrete and specific proposals, and mention those details that the customer perhaps hasn't observed or remembered. At least the customer will know they can count on the help and service of someone who does know what they are doing.

Another thing I recommend, and one that is very important, is never do business without knowing who you are dealing with. This may prevent future problems, especially since nowadays you need plenty of wisdom and caution to avoid being scammed by shady deals, which can create serious problems.

Sales Coaching

CHAPTER THREE

PRODUCT PRESENTATION

*The best advertising is done by
satisfied customers.*

Philip Kotler

I have already talked about real confidence and an in-depth analysis, but I have yet to present the actual product. This last point is the third step in sales. Nevertheless, many salespeople begin with this step instead of the first.

The main reason you visit a customer is to make a sale. Nevertheless, even though that is the primary objective, you cannot overlook the fact that you need to develop the appropriate steps so the customer can prepare himself to buy and be completely satisfied with his purchase. When you go on a long trip, the goal is to reach the destination. But if you don't get the vehicle ready—add fuel, change the oil, take the right route—you might never reach your destination. The same can happen with a sale. If the main goal is to sell the product, but you don't "get your vehicle ready for the road," you don't obtain the proper confidence or carry out a good analysis, you will never reach your objective adequately.

How do you reach that point of making and closing a sale? What does the presentation of the product consist of? Like I have said before, many salespeople start by presenting the product and saying something like: "Hello, my name is such and such; I work for such and such company, and I want to talk about this or that product. Our product..." They then spend about half an hour talking about the product, without having made any previous contact to generate confidence or carry out an analysis. They will become like a fly on a barbecue grill: sure to be burned up in an instant.

How do you present a product? How do you make it interesting? The stages involved in presenting a product are diverse and depend on the goods in question. Nevertheless, there are general guidelines you should follow.

A presentation is not interesting simply because you think it is. There are people who show up to a presentation with a large portfolio of products, papers, laptops and other electronic devices; and the result is not at all interesting. Let me give you an example. A father walked into a store to buy his son a nice toy. He picked out a great box, bought ribbons, wrapped it up, and made a beautiful present. The boy got his gift, opened it, tossed aside the toy, and played with the box instead. This illustrates that what is important to you, may not be important to someone else. This brings us back to the concept of the product. If we go back to the case of the shoe salesman trying to sell a model to a customer, we will remember that the customer was not looking for shoes for himself, but for his wife. So when you go to present a product, the first thing you need to understand is that one thing may be interesting to you and another to your customer. When you show it, do so according to what that product means to your customer, not to you.

FIVE RECOMMENDATIONS FOR MAKING A PRESENTATION INTERESTING

1. PRESENT FROM THE CUSTOMER'S PERSPECTIVE

If there is one concert featuring the Mexican singer Luis Miguel and another featuring the younger Justin Bieber, and if I were to ask my daughter to accompany me to see Luis Miguel, she would almost certainly ask me to go to the Justin Bieber concert instead. She would tell me she doesn't know Luis Miguel; I'd tell her I don't know Justin Bieber. Even if I were to give her a ticket, she wouldn't go to the concert with me. And if she were to give me a ticket, I doubt I would go with her, either. (I'm

> **A presentation is not interesting simply because you think it is**

using both artists as an example with all the respect they deserve.) A presentation is not interesting merely because I think it is. You should remember this so you can avoid falling so much in love with your product that you think the customer will think it's wonderful, too.

Many salespeople speak so fondly about their products that they feel that's all it takes.

The product may be very good, but that does not make a presentation interesting. It may be the best on the market, but what makes a presentation interesting is having a customer ready to listen, and focusing the presentation's points on his needs. The salesperson should have previously discovered these needs along with the customer through an in-depth analysis. For example, if while performing the analysis you discover a customer needs shoes for his wife, then the presentation will only be interesting if you focus on speaking about shoes for his wife—not on the other new models just delivered to the store. As a salesperson, you must be sharp enough to present the detailed aspects that match the customer's interests,

> **The product may be very good, but that does not make a presentation interesting**

and close the presentation on those same aspects, so the presentation doesn't become cliché. There are many sales agents who learn everything there is to know about a product; they learn it by heart. They memorize the presentation but have no way of presenting the product besides what they've learned, which is a mistake because the customer is not necessarily interested in hearing all the information concerning a product. Some customers are in a hurry and only wish to know how much it costs, how long it will last, and when it will be delivered. Others would like to know the size, color, and perhaps some other point; there are still others who only wish to know if it has a warranty or not. The fact is that repeating a product's attributes like a parakeet is not always what makes a presentation interesting for a customer.

The presentation should begin not where you would like it to, but with the most important points the customer indicated during your analysis. I've repeated myself on this point because I want you to learn, not strictly follow the sales manual that tells you step-by-step (one, two, three...) what to do in a presentation without skipping any steps. There are steps that can be left out; don't think that just because you have a portfolio with twenty-five products, you must present them one by one. No! You should start with the one that the customer has shown the most interest in so that your conversation will be of interest to the customer to the extent that you focus on those points.

2. TALK ABOUT THE PRODUCT'S CHARACTERISTICS

Now you may ask, which product? Whichever product your customer is interested in. If he wants a red car, you should talk about the red car; if he wants a pair of tennis shoes, you should talk to him about those tennis shoes. Describe the most relevant points, especially those the customer has shown the most interest in learning about. For example, when describing his interest, if the customer said he wanted a pair of running shoes made of a durable material, start by talking about the materials used in the product being offered, then tell him about the other features.

What are the characteristics of a good product? This is indeed one thing that is defined in a manual, and the manual tells all about the characteristics of a product. Tell about these characteristics once you have the customer's attention. That is the time to say your product is good, "that it has such and such capability, that it has been built out of this or that material, that it has been imported or produced locally, that it is resistant to heat and subject to high quality standards, that it comes in a variety of colors and has been on the market for this amount of years", and so forth.

You should cover every characteristic of the product while keeping track of time, bearing in mind that the customer has already expressed interest in that specific product.

After a certain amount of time, the customer will become distracted, and you should move on to the next step.

That is how you should carry out this small and concise presentation. I say small and concise because you should not waste time or cause your customer to waste time by muddling your presentation with topics that have little to do with the subject at hand. Unless you are selling a NASA rocket or a tank for Afghanistan, you should give yourself three minutes, five at the most, to present the product's characteristics. Why no longer than three minutes? Because during that time, the customer's eyes and ears will be upon you, paying attention to what you say; their body language will tell you up to what point you may keep talking.

Furthermore, the customer may add a series of questions afterward, and these will require extra time to answer. The successful salesperson or adviser knows how to allow for this within a prudent amount of time and does not need to spend hours talking about a product.

3. TALK ABOUT THE PRODUCT'S BENEFITS

Characteristics are one thing, but benefits are something very different. In the previous point, I spoke about a product's characteristics, and how much time you should devote to presenting them. Now you will look at the benefits that your customer will receive from these characteristics. Those benefits could include comfort, warranty, savings due to durability or cost, improved health due to nutritional components, a more active life, or better rest due to its design. Many salespeople mix one with the other; they start talking about characteristics then mention a benefit. When they are asked what the difference is between a characteristic and a benefit, they definitely don't know how to answer.

> **A benefit is what the product's characteristics will generate for the customer**

Characteristics describe what the product is in itself; a benefit is what the product will do for the customer.

For example, it is one thing to say that the car you are selling has a warranty, is from a certain dealership, is good-looking with a brilliant color, and has rugged bodywork. It is another thing to say that with this vehicle you will look like a multimillionaire; your kids will be safer; you can cover a certain amount of miles; your wife will feel like a queen; and you will save on fuel. These are

> **An advantage is what makes one product different from the rest of the competition**

in fact benefits. So what the product is, is one thing, and what it can do for the customer, is another. It is essential for the salesperson to know how to distinguish well between these two points. The best way to do this is by writing them down. Start by making two columns: **characteristics** on one side and **benefits** on the other. Memorize this information so you can handle and play with it during the presentation. If you don't have a good memory, laminate these notes and take them with you so you have those details in hand. Remember that you must start by focusing on whatever the customer has shown the most interest in. Having this list defined beforehand will allow you to be ready and bring it out as needed.

A benefit is what the product's characteristics will generate for the customer.

4. TALK ABOUT THE ADVANTAGES

What is an advantage? An advantage is what makes one

product different from the rest of the competition. Two products may have exactly the same characteristics; however, as a salesperson, you must find reasons why the customer would choose your product, not the competition's. All products have advantages; the difference lies in the focus placed on these advantages, and how well the seller can dig to find them.

If I am going to buy a cell phone, I can look at two similar phones in the store with practically the same general characteristics, but there are some features that can become advantages, that I probably won't be able to detect. So I will need a salesperson, one who is an expert on cell phones and knows these hidden advantages, to show them to me. We can talk about the warranty, the screen's lighting, the wider range of

There are hundreds of features that can be turned into advantages. It is the salesperson's job to discover them and know how to handle them and play them well

colors, or the built-in flashlight. There are hundreds of particular characteristics that aren't related to the cell phone's actual operation that may turn out to be advantages; and in fact, many times, the vendor's service is already an advantage. If two salespeople are selling the same model car but working for different dealerships, the service warranty is almost sure to vary. Thus, the warranty you as a salesperson offer may become an advantage over the warranty offered by the competition, even though the car in question is exactly the same. Now, let's suppose the rival warranty is six months longer than yours, but your company's prestige is greater. That can also be an advantage. Perhaps the other company's warranty offers better terms "on paper," but the reports of complaints from unsatisfied customers, or their negative image may not be so favorable; therefore, your experience and standing in the market will give you the advantage.

There are hundreds of features that can be turned into advantages. It is the salesperson's job to discover them and know how to handle them and play them well.

You cannot assume that people will want what you have simply because it has good characteristics. Sometimes, a consultant offers a product and starts to talk about its characteristics without mentioning the advantages and benefits it offers. For example, one photocopier may be capable of printing 130 pages per minute, another model may print at 120 and another one says it yields 140 pages per minute. If you observe carefully, you will see that the difference between them is ten copies; the standard deviation is plus or minus ten. Many times, a customer will not even hear that difference. He knows the machine will print a hundred and something pages per minute, but maybe he doesn't place too much importance on that particular feature. You believe that since your photocopier can print an additional ten pages per minute, you are gaining ground over the competition; but it may be the customer doesn't care about that. Therefore, you should focus more on the advantages offered by your product than on its characteristics.

> **Your advantages must be convincing, and you should be ready to demonstrate them**

Why mine and not the other? Let's look at the example of multilevel companies. I would recommend making a comparative chart of all the multilevel companies on the market. There are people who speak badly about one company and well about another. They say, "Mine is better than that one." Yet, they don't have any conclusive facts to prove that is true. Why is that? Because they don't research the topic in depth. What do I recommend? My suggestion is that you make a comparative chart of the most powerful multilevel companies on the market; observe them, check into their characteristics, and find out what are the advantages of the one you represent compared to the others. If you present clear advantages while speaking with a client, you will close the deal. It is not a matter of disparaging the competition, because that would be unethical and in very poor taste. It's not a good sign when a salesperson, consultant, or coach resorts to speaking ill of the competition to make a sale. If you are well-acquainted with the advantages of your product over the rest, you don't need to rely on badmouthing; simply compare what you offer in an ethical, professional manner. You know you have great advantages when it comes time to sell your products or affiliate a person into your business, but you should have them at hand. There will be customers who will ask questions, and you should know how to answer them. With the aid of a comparative chart, you can show them why they should join your multilevel company instead of another. I also recommend the use of comparative charts in the insurance business. Making a display that compares all the insurance firms and their products will highlight any advantages over the competition. By showing the features of the various policies, you will make any advantages stand out, and you will be able to demonstrate why your product is the best.

Your advantages must be convincing, and you should be ready to demonstrate them.

I've used the examples of multilevel companies and the

insurance industry to give you a general idea. Actually, for every product that has some competition on the market, the agent should perform a study and draw up this chart. List the five most relevant products, beginning with yours. On an 8½" × 11" or larger sheet of paper, create a chart that is well-organized and understandable. This will allow you to study every product in depth and provide you with a useful breakdown of the information. Remember that you are a salesperson, and destiny may surprise you: today you are selling one product, and tomorrow you may be selling another for the competition. For this reason, be very careful how you express yourself.

> **Knowing the market allows you to become a more complete, well-rounded salesperson who achieves more sales and gains more affiliates**

What can we learn from this? We can learn to study the entire industry; we should not stop to dive into a product without first recognizing the great companies behind every product. When you study an industry, you get more convincing comparisons, and you can say things that are much more pertinent. You can convince your customers in less time, and above all else, you can speak intelligently about your product.

Remember: customers like speaking with people they perceive as intelligent. Don't be a superficial salesperson, spending your whole life selling one product and going no further, without knowing your industry completely, and without knowing everything your product can do for a customer.

5. PRESENT THE APPROPRIATE USE OF THE PRODUCT

There are products that must be used in a specific way, that must be mixed or prepared in a certain manner or in a recommended quantity. Health and chemical products used incorrectly can result in death. The same is true for storage; there are products that have certain storage requirements. Customers always expect that what they purchase will work and work well. If a product does not perform as expected, the blame will fall on that product, tarnishing the company's image. However, what probably happened was that the customer was not given a good explanation of how to use the product.

Knowing the market allows you to become a more complete, well-rounded salesperson who achieves more sales and gains more affiliates.

Let me give an example: A salesman was offering

a customer a stain remover for clothes, which was available in two different forms. The aerosol version called for a certain distance between the clothing and product when applied correctly. In liquid form, the product had to be dissolved in a quantity of water, using an applicator with exact measurements.

The customer decided to purchase both versions, one for use with white clothing and the other for use with colored garments. When it came time to use each product, what the customer did was apply them in the ordinary way that most stain removers on the market are supposed to be used. He sprayed the aerosol directly on a garment and soaked the white clothes in water, applying the liquid stain remover directly as he thought best.

The result was a perfect disaster. The aerosol left a round stain on the garment, and the results on the white clothes from the liquid were not visible. Naturally, the customer concluded that the salesman had tricked him and that the product's manufacturer was a scam.

This led to an immediate customer complaint. Did the customer have a right to complain? Of course he did! The products offered to him did not provide any benefit, and he did not get the desired results. Those same stain removers —aerosol and liquid—from the same manufacturer were offered by another salesman on the same sales force to another customer. That salesman, after having won his customer's trust, and having carried out his analysis, made his presentation in a prudent amount of time, including a demonstration of both products and an explanation of how to use them correctly.

The aerosol demonstration showed how to spray the garments from a specific distance so the product could penetrate the fabric without leaving stains from excessive application. He had the customer try it himself. When demonstrating the liquid version, the salesman used an applicator (which he had given to the customer as a gift) to measure the correct amount of stain remover to a quantity of water indicated by a measurement on the applicator. He sprayed this directly onto the white and colored clothing. The customer thus discovered that he could use either form on any kind of clothing, only that he had to do so using the correct quantities or keeping the required distance between product and garment. In the end, the customer bought both products and was completely satisfied. This salesman closed the sale successfully and gained the loyalty of his customer.

Have you ever heard some people say, "This product is wonderful," while others say (of the same product), "That is completely useless"? I am sure you have. Basically what happens is that somewhere along the line, the product was probably not used in the correct manner.

My father worked for many years as a rice salesman. He had a good number of customers that bought his cereal. This was a quality product, but there was other rice on the market that was similar or even of better quality; even the price was not the most economical.

Nevertheless, my father was an expert in building relationships with his buyers; he knew how to win the loyalty of his consumers. My father had a very unique sales technique: he would cook the rice and take servings to his customers to show them the quality of the product.

The handling of a product can become the main source of complaint by a customer: its storage or where it is kept, moving it, dosage or quantities used, mixing instructions, or how it works.

If the salesperson takes the time to demonstrate the correct use of a product, he will leave the customer more satisfied and will help him avoid needless waste.

Many customers say, "That product is too expensive and doesn't last very long," when what's happening is they're using more than is required. By using the correct measurements, customers can realize that in fact the price they paid is fair and matches the product's capacity.

A product's perceived performance can add or subtract value, and it can also reduce or increase its sales possibilities. No one will keep buying something that does not fulfill expectations, that he does not consider useful or beneficial, that doesn't work or that does not produce savings or create profits. Add to this the reputation that the product creates on the market.

Here is where customer service comes in. Those who only concentrate on selling on one day don't take into account the importance of service. They sell a product, and they couldn't care less how it is used or what results the customer gets. Only when they run into trouble with their sales quotas or goals do they remember that the person they once sold to in the past exists. It may be that in the business of selling intangible goods, such as consulting services, multilevel company products, marketing, insurance policies, vacation plans, and other services, it may not be necessary to demonstrate the proper use or handling of an article or merchandise in the same way as in the

> **If the salesperson takes the time to demonstrate the correct use of a product, he will leave the customer more satisfied and will help him avoid needless waste**

sale of tangible goods. Nevertheless, the services and benefits must be clearly explained in a transparent, convincing manner. Here, the proper use of the product becomes part of the service being offered. This is a greater advantage because you will be selling yourself. If you are offering health insurance, you cannot make a sale without explaining which clinics or health centers the customer can use. The same thing applies to the hotel industry. If you are selling vacation

> **Believe me, tricking people will not help you sell more; as time goes on, it will work against you**

plans or advertising tourist destinations, don't offer more than what the customer will receive. The decision to buy rests solely on the customer, but you will have sold exactly what you offered. If the hotel ends up not being very good, if you move to a much better travel agency, and you contact that old customer, it won't be a bitter case of, "That guy who tricked me is calling." Rather, you will be able to appeal to your honesty and offer a new service. Believe me, tricking people will not help you sell more; as time goes on, it will work against you.

CHAPTER FOUR

AGGRESSIVE CLOSING

Sales Coaching

An aggressive close is one that is carried out now—and in cash.

W hy do so many salespeople fail to close a sale? The first reason is they don't know how to do it. They leave their homes predisposed to thinking that maybe they won't close the sale. Many sellers and sales agents go out well-dressed with their materials ready and organized, but they will accept an "I'll call you later"; "I'll let you know tomorrow"; "Let me consult my wife"; or "I don't have any money today." It is almost as if there was a previous mental programming to accept that other people have control over their sales, instead of the opposite. In other words, there are people who have made it a rule in their minds and practices that a sale is not closed on the same day; they have to go back and keep trying. They take it as the norm for the customer to say, "Come back later," so they close their briefcases and leave, saying, "I'll talk with you tomorrow," or "I'll come back and visit again next week." They trust their customer's words, but I can tell you that is a huge mistake! Besides that, there are many leaders who train their sales force to get used to closing sales over several visits. They prepare them mentally, and they accept that their salespeople may close a deal two, three, or four days after having initiated the process. If they make this a normal practice, sometimes it may take them up to three months to close a sale.

The first mistake a leader makes is believing that sales are closed the day after.

When a leader believes this, the entire company believes it and its sales force believes it as well; it becomes a rule, which certainly does not result in aggressive closings. You may ask, what is an aggressive close? An aggressive close is one that is made now! —and in cash. When I go out to sell, I am not setting out to sell illusions or products; I am setting out to close sales. When I am selling something, I am completely convinced that what I am offering is worth buying; I am confident that the price paid by my customers is fair. I am also convinced my customers need what they are buying from me, so, since they need it, it's good for them to have it and pay a fair price. I have complete confidence that there is nothing stopping them from buying it now—and in cash. Why should I have to

> **The first mistake a leader makes is believing that sales are closed the day after**

believe they can't purchase it now and in cash? Why should I go out programmed to think that the decision belongs only to the customer? And why should I go out prepared to accept it and grovel at the customer's feet? "Buy my product. Please buy my product." No! Products cost what they cost.

If a car costs $25,000, it's because it's worth $25,000, and all the cars it is competing with should have approximately the same value. There is no reason for you to feel ashamed that someone will buy a car from you for that price; it's up to them to have the money to pay for it. It is not your job to find them the money, unless the company stipulates that financing must be arranged by the salesperson, or if the customer himself asks for financing. Generally speaking, the customer must have the ability to pay, and it is your job to discover their ability. What you need to understand is that this customer needs a vehicle, and you will help him get one—but he is the one who must pay for it. You cannot approach the situation thinking: "Poor gentleman, he will have to find $25,000. That's a lot of money!" No, that is not your role. It's one thing to guide and help customers, but another thing entirely to feel sorry for them.

On one occasion, a multilevel adviser commented about a prospective candidate she had and was going to affiliate in her organization. What got my attention was when she told me: "I'm thinking of helping him with 50 percent of the registration fee because I don't think he has the money."

Immediately I asked her, "How do you know he doesn't have the money?"

"I don't know," she answered. "His appearance tells me he doesn't have a lot of resources available." That is a huge mistake. You should not do that—unless the person is a close relative. What's more, close relatives who become our customers are the most problematic of all. Believe me! By doing that, you are not giving your product the value that it's worth. And, when something costs a person nothing, they simply do not assign it its due importance.

Paying a fair price for something is what makes it valuable.

If you are inclined to think that a person has no money, you are not really understanding what it means to sell. Selling is the act of giving someone else what they need in exchange for a price they must pay—and in this day and age, products and services are paid for with money. If people need something, they must be willing to pay for it. This is not something that should frighten or embarrass you as a salesperson.

Let's take a look at a much simpler type of sale. In many countries, but especially in Latin America, gasoline is sold at gas stations by attendants. In the United States and in other places, there is what is called self-serve: you pull up to a pump, pay for your purchase, and pump your gasoline. Let's imagine you arrive at a gas station with an empty fuel tank. The pump attendant opens your vehicle's gas cap but doesn't say much

<<<<<<<<<<<<<<<<<<<<<<<<<<<<<<<<<<<<<<<<<

Paying a fair price for something is what makes it valuable

<<<<<<<<<<<<<<<<<<<<<<<<<<<<<<<<<<<<<<<<<

except to ask how many gallons you want. He's not interested in why you're going to pump that quantity. He will not ask why you aren't saving half of your twenty dollars for lunch; he simply isn't interested! So don't waste your time explaining that because the attendant will not dispute it with you, and he won't be inclined to think that perhaps you don't have enough money on you. All he knows is that he sells gasoline, that you came to the gas station to buy it, and that you must pay immediately for the gallons you've purchased. He won't be thinking that perhaps you only dropped by to check out the prices and come back another day. No! Everything is already set up so customers can show up with their cars, park in front of a pump, pay for the fuel purchase, pump that fuel into the car, and see you later! The point is, you and the attendant don't go into a discussion of whether you will pump the fuel or not, or whether you will pump today but pay tomorrow. We're talking about an intentional sale, and that is how sales work: you should buy what you need, and you must be willing to pay for it. If you are the one selling, the same principle applies.

◇◇◇◇◇◇◇◇◇◇◇◇◇◇◇◇◇◇◇◇◇◇◇◇◇◇◇◇

If he doesn't pay now and in cash, it won't be considered an aggressive close

◇◇◇◇◇◇◇◇◇◇◇◇◇◇◇◇◇◇◇◇◇◇◇◇◇◇◇◇

It is not about a convenience; it is not about letting you know later, or getting back to you next week. If the customer has decided the product is good (after having taken all the pertinent steps and being convinced he needs it, and it will bring him benefits) then he must pay its fair price; he should buy right now and pay cash. If he doesn't pay now and in cash, it won't be considered an aggressive close. The close may be made later on, but it will be just another close and never an aggressive close. Aggressive closes produce impressive results.

If you are selling something to someone, the other person needs to reach a level of understanding that moves him or her to buy the product at that moment—and pay for it immediately.

Next we will see how that is done. How can you make immediate sales? How do you convince a customer he must pay at that moment and that this contract should be closed right away? By the time the customer reaches this point, he must be aware and convinced that he wants and needs the product. You have already created that level of awareness, and the customer must have a clear idea of how much he will be paying. If you are afraid of revealing this or are hesitant to press the point, the customer will perceive it. If he realizes he can wait until tomorrow, he will do so. If the customer senses that he can overcome the salesperson, he will; and if he senses that he can get rid of him easily, he will.

Years ago, I went to claim prizes that were being given out by a travel agency. This company was dedicated to selling travel packages, and it used vacation prizes as a way to attract potential customers. Back then, I was still young, and the salespeople had offered my family and me a weekend getaway in a hotel. They asked me a series of important questions to qualify me, but I lied on many of the answers, thinking I was smarter than they. On the question about my annual income, I made a calculation of what I thought would be attractive in terms of salary to qualify for the prize and put that on the questionnaire. I stated that I made around $5,000 a month when my salary didn't even amount to $2,000. I sat there listening to all the information and waited to receive my free weekend getaway. Afterward, the salesman approached me and said, "Very well then, let's talk business. The price for a lifetime plan is $21,000."

I responded, "Wow, a lifetime plan!"

He went on, "Yes, a lifetime plan. For the rest of your life, you and your family will have the opportunity to go on vacations with this plan."

I kept looking at him and then proposed, "Great! Let me consult with my wife."

The salesman immediately asked me a question I have never forgotten: "If I gave you this plan free of charge, would you consult with your wife? I'm sure you wouldn't. Do you know why I think so? Because I think you have a money problem. Am I right?"

I realized I had fallen into a trap. I had to admit that my problem was indeed the money. My pride and self-esteem were really hurt, but this salesman was completely right. He was well aware of what was going on. He was totally sure he was not going to give me anything for free; I was there to pay for that vacation plan. I was the one who had no idea what was going on. You know what? Nothing is free; everything has a price. Any time you receive something, you can be sure there is some interest attached to it. In this case, it was in the interest of selling or getting something in exchange.

The sales associate then said this, "I'm obligated to fill out a report about this deal I began with you. So with your permission, I would like to speak with

Nothing is free; everything has a price

my manager. I must certify that I am doing a good job. My company needs to know that I spent my time working, and the main reason you didn't buy anything today is because you lack the money to do so. It isn't because the product is unsuitable or because you have misunderstood anything." He undoubtedly kept hurting my self-esteem, and as a young man without experience, I had no idea how I was going to get out of this predicament.

The sales manager showed up and approached me, "Are you Mr. Astacio?"

"Yes," I responded.

"You came to purchase a plan, did you not?"

I was bold enough to respond, "Yes, of course."

"OK," said the manager. "The salesman has told me the main reason you will not be buying is that you don't have the money. Is that true?"

I had no choice but to confess, "That is true."

I ended up leaving that store completely ashamed. Nevertheless, I learned something from this episode. If in that instant I had been able to find the money, I would have bought that vacation plan just because of the damage done to my pride. The salesman had put me into a situation where without a doubt I would have purchased it from him—if only to show him I was capable of buying. That salesman was trying to make an aggressive close, and although it may sound uncomfortable to admit it, the truth is, that is the goal. You cannot go to a place of business believing that you are the owner of the entire negotiation. You are the owner of 50 percent of the negotiation, and whoever is supplying a product for you in exchange is the owner of the other

> **If a customer gives you a sign he wishes to close right away, close the deal immediately; take advantage of the moment**

50 percent. Therefore, a buyer must pay a fair price for something valuable. The aggressive close is based on this, on being aware that things cost what they cost. A buyer must pay the fair price for something in cash—today, not tomorrow or Monday.

THREE CHARACTERISTICS OF AN AGGRESSIVE CLOSE

1. IT IS DONE AT ONCE

The first characteristic of an aggressive close is that it is done at once, immediately. For this to happen, you have to wait for what is known in the sales world as buying signals. Customers give off signals that indicate they wish to end the conversation and close the deal. Salespeople who aren't paying attention don't know how to manage this situation well but should learn to do so.

Many times the customer will give a signal he is willing to close the deal, but the seller keeps talking. It is almost as if he's afraid of reaching that point, and so he starts looking for something to keep entertaining the customer. The longer the seller talks, the more likely he is to make mistakes. If a customer gives you a sign he wishes to close right away, close the deal immediately; take advantage of the moment. You cannot say to the customer, "Wait. Let me tell you more about this." Believe me, I have seen cases where the seller thinks he needs to say it all, absolutely everything, and overlooks the signals the customer is giving to indicate he's ready to close the deal. When the customer gives these signals, it is because he is sufficiently convinced and has seen what he's interested in, which is enough. Anything beyond that will be a post-sale service; but first, you must close the deal.

A buying signal often has to do with the words a customer uses or the attention he fixes on you or your product. Some questions are buying signals. For example: How can I pay for that? How much does it cost exactly? When will it be delivered? What other colors are available? What size is it? These kinds of questions are directly related to the product. The customer is showing a particular interest, and that is why he is asking specific questions. When these signals are given, you should focus on answering by guiding the customer toward closing the deal.

Remember that questions are the master key.

If a customer asks how he or she should pay for the product, never answer, "However you wish." Every time a customer poses a question, the seller must stop for a moment to analyze it. Normally, closing questions are not answered with a statement, but with another question. For example, if the customer asks how to pay, the seller should ask a question in return, "How would you like to pay?"

Notice that it is an entirely different dynamic. By responding with a question, you are doing two things: First, you are confirming that what you are offering has a price, a value, and it really must be paid. Second, you are confirming that the customer is not going to make a future purchase, but is taking it as fact that he has already acquired it.

Remember that questions are the master key

This is a way to induce your customer's brain to fix in his mind the idea that he will pay for it. From that will come the answer indicating how he wants to pay, be it cash or payments. That confession is highly significant. We lawyers talk about personal confessions; which is why it is important for the customer himself to be the one who says, "I wish to pay for it this way or that way."

Answering a customer's question does not create a commitment.

If you answer, "It can be paid in four payments," the customer will surely respond with, "That's fine," which doesn't reveal or imply an agreement. But reeling them in with another question will make them confess directly how they are going to pay, which is admitting the fact they will acquire the product.

When these signs show up, don't run ahead or rush things. Once the customer states how he wishes to pay, follow that up with another question, "If I can get you an additional discount, would you pay in cash?" Now you have

Payment plans are not a sales tool; they are an alternative tool

two options: if the customer responds with Yes, he will close the deal immediately; please don't argue any further. Take advantage of the moment and close that sale. If the customer claims, "Well, I might not be able to pay the entire amount right now," don't give him time; immediately come back with something like, "Well, I could try to set up a payment plan. If I do, will you buy the product now?" What I do is use the customer's affirmation to lead them to a confirmation of the sale. If I make the effort to get the payment plan, he has already told me he will close the deal today, not tomorrow. So next I call my supervisor or manager and let him know that I've found an opportunity for him to take advantage of at that moment.

Even if the seller has payment plans available, he should not rely on that tool at first. If a customer can pay for something at once, why wait three months? Payment plans are not a sales tool; they are an alternative tool.

Imagine that a robber has broken into your house, and you have a pistol hidden under your pillow. The pistol has no bullets. You pull out your weapon and point it at the robber. If the robber were to ask, "Is that pistol loaded?" What would you tell him? That it doesn't have any bullets? Of course, you wouldn't tell him that. You would never reveal such a secret. With or without bullets, you are going to use that pistol to chase away the robber. The pistol had no bullets, but that information was for you to know only; the robber had no reason to know that. A salesperson should learn to handle the information that belongs to him. Regardless of how insignificant or irrelevant a piece of information may seem, the customer may assign great importance to it if he is aware of it. Any additional benefits can become a tool to use after observing buying signals; therefore, don't reveal them all at once. Be smart.

> **Any additional benefits can become a tool to use after observing buying signals; therefore, don't reveal them all at once—be smart**

But what if you don't see any buying signals? How do you close the deal? Sometimes the buying signals are not present, or they are not easy to see. Since the deal should be closed at the right moment, if the customer does not give the signals, what the seller should do is lead them in that direction. Once the seller has connected with the customer through an in-depth analysis, and has taken each step including giving an interesting presentation, the customer will have shown a particular interest in one point of the proposal; that is when the closing process must be started. The process is initiated by the salesperson's master key: questions.

Start by asking questions that will allow you to reach that closing point. For example: When would you like to have the product delivered to you? What day of this week should I bring you your ticket for the next convention? What do you plan to do once you have signed this contract? How would you like to pay for it: cash, check, or credit card? The customer's own answer will seal the deal. This is known as an alternative choice close. It doesn't matter what the customer responds, the answer he provides can lead him toward saying Yes.

A salesperson can't spend all day waiting for signals.

Nevertheless, I must say there will be customers who will have objections. Some may say, "Now hold on a minute; I'm not buying yet"; or perhaps, "I didn't say I was going to pay that." Customers like these are not necessarily saying they will never buy; they may be saying, "Perhaps not now, but later on." Many customers say No, but even they don't understand their own response. Try to guide your customer toward a brief analysis of what they have answered; and, as always, this must be done by using questions. Guide the conversation; give the customer the opportunity to tell you the real reason, what he really thinks.

2. IT IS DONE WITHOUT BEING AFRAID OF WHAT THE CUSTOMER HAS TO PAY

There are many salespeople who are afraid of telling their customers the price of their products, which underestimates their customers and their capacity to make decisions. They are also underestimating the power of emotions and neuroscience. When a person is excited about something, even if they don't have the money, they will make the sacrifice to get it—because of their excitement, and besides, things have value, as we have seen several times. When this happens, it is generally because the salesperson is thinking to himself: If I don't have a million dollars, I doubt the customer is capable of having it.

There are salespeople and consultants, who after

naming their price, offer payment plans, which, again, underestimates the customers' ability to pay. What ends up happening is that the salesperson believes the price is a great deal of money, so they pass on their thought to the customer. You know what? There is no such thing as too much money. Angelina Jolie bought an island for Brad Pitt. I don't know how much it cost her, but I am sure it was a few million dollars. She wanted an island for her husband, and she knew she had to pay for it. Since she knew what she wanted, she surely had an estimate of the cost involved.

Fear is not a good counselor

What you need to understand is that if a person wishes to purchase a fifteen-story building, they will buy it already having a good idea of what it is worth. So if you are the real estate agent, and you tell them the price, don't be alarmed. You aren't the one buying the building. Just think this way: Your customer has the ability to manage the millions of dollars the building is worth. Your customer has the money available. And they have clearly decided what they want to do.

Fear is not a good counselor. When giving a price, be firm and minimize that sum in your own mind. Start thinking that a million dollars is nothing for that building; there are buildings that cost much more. So when it comes time to reveal the price, you won't be beating around the bush. Don't say it with trepidation or shifty eyes, and don't use phrases like, "Well..., but..., what happens is..." Fear is not a good counselor. Fear makes you sympathize so much you immediately offer all the payment arrangements you can give — and that is a mistake. Who told you the customer is seeking help with the payment? He has a million dollars; he has decided to buy a building that's worth that much, and he has the means to

> **If everything has its price, then there is no reason for you to be afraid when stating what it's worth**

write a check. It is important that you keep this very much in mind. No matter how much something you are selling may cost, you should never be afraid. It is better to minimize the prices; tell the customer, in clear terms, what the price of the product is and that he should pay for it right now. That is the watchword.

If everything has its price, then there is no reason for you to be afraid when stating what it's worth. If it costs a million dollars, then it costs a million dollars.

Credit terms should be requested by the customer, not

offered by the seller as soon as possible; that is not his job. Not all customers have the same ability to pay; that much is clear. Nevertheless, the salesperson must wait for the customer to be the one to solicit credit. The same is true for discounts. Wait until it really is necessary to offer as a last resort to close a sale. Most companies, if not all of them, pay their sales forces based on amounts collected, not sales; therefore, the less money you collect, the less commission you will receive. If you really want to make money, you should strive to have your customers pay in full, or the greatest possible percentage of the initial purchase.

This is where the subject of decision comes into play, which is why you should put everything on the table when talking to people

The question of price is always present, as are other related questions: How can I pay for it? When do I have to pay for it? At what point during delivery should I pay for it? There are hundreds of similar questions that have to do with prices and payment. If the customer responds with: "That is too expensive"; or "Let me think about it"; or "Let me consult with my wife," always remember to ask: "And if I gave it to you free, would you still consult with her?" Their answer will show you there is an economic factor involved, so don't avoid the subject. Talk with your customer; explain that you know what is going on. But touch on the subject as delicately and professionally as you can, unlike what happened to me. When there are no other options, that is when you open the door to any financing opportunities you can provide. If the customer wants and needs the product, then they should get it. With the way the economy twists and turns, today they may not be solvent, and thus, not able to purchase with cash right now. Nevertheless, tomorrow they may be able to.

Of course, you should be careful to explain that this is an opportunity that is being offered due to this current circumstance. In this way, the customer won't become accustomed to paying with credit if he can pay in full. Remember: you will lose income if this happens.

This is where the subject of decision comes into play, which is why you should put everything on the table when talking to people. There are certain individuals who are experts at wasting a salesperson's time— that's something that cannot be denied. They believe that wasting time is part of a salesperson's job, and that it doesn't mean anything. I've heard some people say, "That's your job." These people have adopted that behavior because they are accustomed to dealing with salespeople who have come to them without any kind of demands or control. When a person is being sold something they need, if they are going to buy, they have to be perfectly aware that its price is what it costs and they have to pay it. Sometimes, time is spent on customers who end up not buying anything, so it's important for you to value and manage your time.

3. SHOW YOU ARE ENTIRELY PREPARED TO CLOSE

The salesperson, adviser, or agent must be completely prepared to close the deal, and by this, I mean having all the related products and materials in hand. For example, if a person who works in multilevel marketing visits a prospective recruit, they should have in hand their sponsorship kit and samples of the main products sold, at least one of each. This means salespeople must make an investment. If you haven't invested in materials, you will be telling your client, "OK, wait for me here. I will bring you the contract to sign in an hour." Imagine that! You are showing that you are not at all prepared to close at that moment.

People purchase things emotionally and later justify their purchases rationally.

When people go out to buy something, all of their emotions are involved. As you provide more information, the customer will become more excited and reach an emotional climax, which will allow you to close the deal. If you let that emotional climax simmer down and disappear, the customer will go home to talk to his wife, friend, or children, who will ask him, "Why do you want to get involved in that?" Therefore, the salesperson should be ready to close the deal at the right moment, usually in the first contact of the sale.

I have known some very prepared salespeople who were ready to close at the right moment; but I've also known many, who, when asked if they could close immediately,

People purchase things emotionally and later justify their purchases rationally

confessed it would be impossible because they lacked an application, pen, or some other basic item. The reason these salespeople were unprepared is that they had been programmed to close the deal in several visits. I encourage you never to do this as a rule, because it isn't right. Doing this will cause you to lose many contracts.

The initial contact produces a magical, emotional moment—*a high point* that will be very hard to replicate.

If you lose the chance to close on that first visit, it

means you were not prepared to do so. Trying to get another opportunity like that could cost you a great deal of time.

Let me tell you another story. On one occasion, I went to close a life insurance deal. I was dealing with the customer for an hour. We got to the final stage and closed the deal; but when the time came to pay, the customer ended the conversation, saying, "I have a problem. I don't have the checks here. They're in the company building." This gentleman was wearing shorts and in no hurry to leave the comfort of his home. But I knew that if I didn't take advantage of the emotion in that moment, it would never be the same. So I said, "Very well, let's do something. Let's go to your office. I'll take you there so you won't have to bother driving, and then you can find your checkbook." He was hesitating. I explained to him that today he was insurable; we didn't know about tomorrow. I asked him several confirming questions to keep him excited, and since he responded positively to everything, I insisted, "Well, let's go. Don't worry; that's what I'm here for." The gentleman agreed to come with me. He went into his office, found and signed the check, then handed it to me. While handing the check over, he said, "You should wait three or four days to cash it. I don't have the funds in my account just yet." You might be thinking, a check without funds means nothing! However, that is not the case. If you close a deal with a customer, and he signs a postdated check, that customer now has a different commitment to you. Now the issue is one of payment, not a sale. In my case, three weeks went by while I tried to confirm if I could deposit the check; I kept calling him so he would authorize me. If it took me three weeks to cash that check, what would have happened if I had left without a check when he'd told me he didn't have one at home? Would he really have purchased the insurance? You can be sure he wouldn't have done so. Maybe it would have taken me three months to meet with him again. That is why we salespeople should always be prepared. Imagine if I hadn't had fuel in my car that day. How could I have taken him to his office? Be ready to accept the customer's decision with all the resources required: a pen, an application, a kit, a delivery list, or whatever is necessary to finalize things right here, right now.

MANAGE YOUR OWN EMOTIONS

People are allergic to having things sold to them, but they love buying. It may seem like a contradiction, but the human brain fixates on a mindset that if the person needs something, he has to have it. That is the salesperson's job: to make the customer see that the product he has is necessary, adequate, and good for him. Nowadays, there is talk of the neuroscience of sales and of emotional intelligence. These concepts have demonstrated that the more influence you have over your customer's thoughts, the more success you will have. That's why it's important to win the confidence of your customer, perform a good analysis, and make a presentation that's interesting and timely for the customer, with masterful questions, so that when the emotional climax is reached, the deal can be closed

◇◇◇◇◇◇◇◇◇◇◇◇◇◇◇◇◇◇◇◇◇◇◇◇◇

It is important for salespeople to know how to manage their own emotions because their emotions have a direct influence on those of their customers

◇◇◇◇◇◇◇◇◇◇◇◇◇◇◇◇◇◇◇◇◇◇◇◇◇

aggressively. Only share as much information as is necessary because an excess of information triggers the rational part of the brain, which displaces the emotional part, which is a sale's greatest ally.

Emotional intelligence is not limited to the customer's emotions but also includes your own emotions.

It is important for salespeople to know how to manage their own emotions because their emotions have a direct influence on those of their customers. Have you ever observed how soap operas or movies work on the emotions of the viewer? When there is an episode on the screen, you feel like it is happening to you, not to the actor. This happens because the actors convey emotions; they are experts at doing so. That is why as a salesperson, you must be extremely careful about the emotions you convey; customers will pick up on any anxiety and will connect it to their own lives. Positive emotions attract people, and of course that means customers. Negative emotions have the opposite effect.

If a salesperson is perceived as being a problem solver, it will enhance his relationship with his customer.

Learn to manage your emotions so that they help you, not hinder you. Perception goes hand in hand with emotions; depending on what you convey, that is what the customer's perception will be. People who are perceived as being exhausted and without hope are not capable of motivating others. Are you an insurance agent, a multilevel sponsor, a car salesman, a kitchen wares seller, an advertising sales representative, or someone engaged in any other sales activity? Work your emotions. A person who talks about success cannot give the opposite impression. I like the fact that multilevel advisers dress well; their impeccable clothing suggests a sense of security. Those who are not in a good emotional state do not display passion for what they are doing. However, when they radiate vitality and energy, they will be able to break through a number of barriers.

DON'T FORGET ABOUT CUSTOMER SERVICE

There are innovative commercial strategies focused on seeking customers' satisfaction, based on knowledge of the human brain and emotions. Customer loyalty is covered in these strategies. This is why it is of utmost importance to achieve empathy between you and your customers and to reinforce that empathy after the close with excellent service so that the relationship will last through the years. With your service, you will build a reputation not only for a brand, but for yourself. The customer will form a perception of value and have a more favorable opinion of you. Customers who are satisfied with the service given are essentially subscribers, frequent buyers who will eventually become loyal customers. This also has the benefit of generating referrals; because of their experience with your service, they will recommend you to their acquaintances and relatives.

So, once you have closed a sale, you should not forget about your customer. Don't wait for them to call you. Showing a particular interest in them will help you gain ground and earn their loyalty. If you make a habit of calling your customers to give them your regards, the next time they think of buying something, they will think of you. What's more, any time they wish to buy a product—even if it has nothing to do with the brand you represent—they might still ask you to recommend someone who can provide that service. This is because of what we've covered regarding emotions based on experiences. Since he has received excellent service from you, the customer understands that as his adviser, you can recommend someone who works in the same manner, even if you don't share the same field.

Throughout my years of experience, regardless of the industry involved, I have seen that as time goes on, loyal customers become friends. It doesn't matter what organization you happen to be in, if you have formed lasting relationships, they will continue being your customers. This is because human beings display a sense of things belonging to them. So insurance agents won't

> **Customers who are satisfied with the service given are essentially subscribers, frequent buyers who will eventually become loyal customers**

be just an agent, they will be my agent; the uplines won't be just an upline, they will be my upline. It is the same with doctor-patient relationships. You don't generally go around switching doctors. You stick with one health professional because he already knows everything about your health.

Good service implies that as a salesperson, you must be ready to supply the required merchandise on time. For example, if you sell cosmetics, it can be safely assumed that you have an idea how long the customer's product will last. Before it runs out, you should contact the customer so they can replace it. A service or sale should have an expiration date, and you should be awaiting that date. When contacting your customers, don't do it so often you bore them; it is not about hounding them. You should be careful to avoid that, since there are salespeople who border on the unbearable. Remember that people need their space. Not all customers will be as open as some, so try to get a sense of their rhythm.

◇◇◇◇◇◇◇◇◇◇◇◇◇◇◇◇◇◇◇◇◇◇◇◇◇◇◇◇

In summary, satisfying the needs and expectations of your customers through excellent service assures their permanence and loyalty

◇◇◇◇◇◇◇◇◇◇◇◇◇◇◇◇◇◇◇◇◇◇◇◇◇◇◇◇

Certain restaurants provide us with an example of service. You may visit an establishment that offers an excellent menu with exquisite food. But if the order takes too long to arrive, or the music is deafening, you won't be coming back, regardless of how good the food may be. In contrast, some places, with a less varied menu, offer a warm environment and good music; they are effective at bringing out orders on time and making their customers feel well-cared-for. My wife loves Peruvian food, and I was very excited to take her to a restaurant that specialized in that cuisine. However, our evening was terrible. We ordered at 9:00 p.m. and our food took an hour and a half to arrive, and even then, some dishes never came. As a result, we decided we would not return. Several months later, I took her to a new restaurant that offered the same cuisine. Though their menu was not as extensive as the previous restaurant's, the service was stupendous.

In summary, satisfying the needs and expectations of your customers through excellent service assures their permanence and loyalty.

Every once in a while, surprise your customers with gifts or promotions; it is not all about money. If you work with beauty products, offer them a facial. If you promote multilevel plans, give them a good book. If you sell automobiles, give them an air freshener, a steering wheel cover, or something else that will make them feel you are thinking about them.

Have you ever seen a salesperson arguing with their customer over a complaint? I have. If the customer expresses any complaint, pay attention to him; make the customer feel your approval in what he is saying. Complaints and suggestions are not bad; they should be taken into account because they help you grow and become better.

I have now covered the four essential steps that will help you become a successful seller. These four steps have been elaborated so that you may have enough tools at your disposal to meet your goals.

As always, I appreciate any of your comments, which are a great encouragement to my team and me.

You may write to us at info@motivationteam.org dioastacio@yahoo.com

Social networks:

Twitter: @dioastacio
Instagram: Dioastacio
FB: Pastor Dío Astacio

Website: www.motivationteam.org
Follow our YouTube channel: Dío Astacio

God bless your life!